GENERO
FOR TH

"Anusha is a welcome addition to the healing tools assisting the energetic shift we are now undergoing. Read, use and enjoy."

Judy Hall ~ Author of 'The Crystal Bible I & II'

"This is a lovely gentle book that will introduce seekers to a journey of discovery that was undertaken with hope, joy and enthusiasm. I feel this book is an important stepping stone for those trying to move forward on their path towards harmony and enlightenment."

Thea Holly ~ Channeller & Author of 'Listening to Trees'

"This book is a joy to read, full of love and warmth in Patsi's own true style. It reaches out, combining personal experiences with an account of how Anusha came in to being as a healing system. It clearly shows with words and diagrams how to use Anusha on yourself or others, whether you are a newcomer to healing or experienced in other areas. A book to refer to again and again."

Sarah Lewis ~ Person-Centred Counsellor

"I feel that this book is an excellent, thorough, informative text and handbook for Anusha Healing."

LeelaLight ~ Spiritual Teacher & Life Guide

"Too often when you read an autobiographical book, seeking help, you're left feeling, Well that worked fine for him/her, but I'm none the wiser as to how to help 'me'. In this case you'll discover a cohesive, easy to understand, step by step guide to self-healing."

Jenny Smedley ~ Author of 'Soul Angels'

"I was moved by the passion, warmth and wisdom emanating from every page of this inspiring book. I fully endorse the central message of letting go of fear and embracing love."

Colin Tipping ~ Author of 'Radical Forgiveness' & founder of The Institute for Radical Forgiveness Therapy and Coaching

"This book is beautifully and passionately written, with a sense of love that came flowing out of the pages. I felt uplifted and warm just reading it. For anyone who is interested in making our world a better place to be in, surrounded by love, then this is a 'must read'."

Julia Webb-Harvey ~ Counsellor & Author of 'Hurt'

"As an Anusha healer it is brilliant to have all the information we need in one book."

Giles Ayling ~ Anusha & Reiki Healer

"This is a remarkable book, intelligently written. Anusha enables us to connect with the higher frequencies of star energy and is complementary with energies such as Reiki. Connecting with Anusha adds a new dimension to your healing practice truly unlocking your healing potential."

Helen K. Emms ~ Peak Performance Specialist & Author of 'Changing Mindsets & Developing Spirit'

"Patsi is compassionate, truly loving and has remarkable empathy for others. Her unique qualities are portrayed in this astounding and beautifully written book. Exciting! As the mystery of Anusha is revealed."

Liz Everett ~ Anusha Healer/Teacher & Author of 'An Inner Light That Shines So Bright'

"I just love this book for its elegant simplicity in describing not only how the system re-emerged but the ways in which the symbols can be used and their power increased by interaction with each other."

Frankie (Frances) Free ~ Counsellor, Healer & Hypnotherapist

"To essentially be the conduit for the reincarnation of an entire celestial healing system is amazing. Even having access to the material on the printed page is in itself healing."

Vincent Martin ~ Healer & Visionary

"Patsi's journey to Anusha is truly inspiring. The methods she suggests for working with this vibrant energy healing system are exciting and unique. This book is your first step towards an amazing journey home to your Self. Just follow the star..."

Liz Murdoch ~ Crystal/Reiki Healer
& Anusha Master Teacher

"This book exudes warmth, compassion and integrity as the pieces of the Anusha jigsaw fall into place with a satisfying synchronicity. I encourage you to actively engage with the symbols and meditations, embracing their healing power."

Barbara Thomas ~ Counsellor, Sound Healer
& Anusha Master Teacher

Anusha Healing

Shining a
Beacon of
Love in
Changing
Times

PATSI HAYES

lip

First published in 2010 by:

Live It Publishing
27 Old Gloucester Road
London, United Kingdom.
WC1N 3AX
www.liveitpublishing.com

Cover Design, Artwork & Photography by Greg Pike

All enquiries should be addressed to Live It Publishing.

This book is designed to provide accurate and authoritative
information in regard to the subject matter covered.
It is sold with the understanding that neither the author nor
publisher are giving specific diagnostic or treatment advice. If
psychological, emotional or physical treatment is needed, the
services of a competent professional should be sought.

ISBN 978-1-906954-13-0 (pbk)

Sending you peace, harmony, joy
and abundance ...
Shine your light!
Warm love,
Parsi
xxx

DEDICATION

I dedicate this book to all those who find
themselves drawn to heal themselves and others.
Open your hearts and allow your love to flow.

CONTENTS

A Personal Note

Have you ever felt that something was missing from your life? Something you haven't quite been able to put your finger on ... a vague something, intangible, ethereal ... something you just haven't been able to grasp? Have you felt unfulfilled, dissatisfied, that your life lacked purpose and meaning? Have you asked yourself the age-old question, "What am I here for?" in the belief that the answer is somewhere out there, perhaps to be found on the lips of a seer or deep in the hallowed pages of an ancient tome?

I'd searched for many decades to find meaning in my life, at times truly believing I'd found my purpose only to be confounded by an unexpected sinking sense of dissatisfaction. I remember clearly sharing this feeling with my mother ~ that I'd never felt remotely close to a sense of fulfilment ~ and watched her crumpled face display the sadness and disappointment that reflected my own.

This is how I felt before I came upon Anusha healing.

Since then I've been inspired and uplifted, transported to a place of conviction that my purpose is to share the love, knowledge and wisdom that Anusha contains. My purpose is to heal myself and to extend this truly amazing healing energy to others. Through the various ups and downs that have featured in my recent life, I have held this conviction close to my heart. It is with this optimistic sense of serving the highest good that I share with you, from my heart to yours, all that Anusha healing has to offer.

INTRODUCTION

We are living in momentous times.

The good news is that consciousness is rising exponentially. Multitudes of people around the world are waking up to the realisation that acquiring material wealth in greedy, desperate, competitive and ruthless ways doesn't fill the gaping holes. Ultimately, it just makes those holes bigger.

The better news is that our individual and combined hearts are opening to the truism that all we actually need is love.

There is no bad news!

Whatever's unfolding right here and now is perfect and part of the Divine plan!

Anusha healing caresses the agonising ache of emptiness, pointlessness, and meaninglessness that many souls are feeling at this time. It fills that hollow space as it begins to nurture, to nourish, to facilitate the flow of self-healing, self-love, self-acceptance. More than anything, it brings a deep and satisfying sense of inner peace and calm, a connection to our true wealth ~ our ability to love, cherish and extend compassion to others, and ourselves, unconditionally. It provides a lifeline to that expansive wisdom and knowledge that nestles forgotten and untapped within each and every one of us.

With Anusha comes the realisation that we have been looking for fulfilment in all the wrong places, that we can liberate ourselves by simply letting go of this pressing and frantic need to search. We need do only one fundamental thing ~ come home to ourselves, come home to love!

This book shares with you the expansive healing ability of Anusha with the invitation to use it for yourself and others ~ for your family, friends, your community and, ultimately, the Earth. It invites you to become part of this Anusha community, to share your love, to feel connected in peace, hope and harmony to all and everything on this planet.

We are truly living in momentous times!

PHASE 1

EMBARKING
ON THE QUEST

Pacing the Sand

Nomada ~ The Master Symbol

I struggled to know where to start this book, which part of my Anusha journey to share with you first. So much has happened, my life has changed immeasurably and, when I take a panoramic view, much of it seems really complex and incredible. Perhaps I'll start by saying that, back in 2004 when I first encountered this new energy, I was very open to and connected with my intuition. I understood that nothing is coincidental, that things that apparently happen by chance have deep significance and meaning. Indeed, throughout my life I have been gifted with a sixth sense, which was about to be working overtime!

I guess it all began when my friend, Kate, and I were meandering through Glastonbury, having decided that we wouldn't allow ourselves to spend any more money.

We were walking past a second hand bookstall when a book 'leapt out' and fell to the floor in our path. Looking back we were not really surprised but understood that this unusual event had happened for a reason. The book was quite clearly calling to be read, so I paid the modest £2 and tucked it in my bag, only to forget about it for a while.

Shortly afterwards, on Easter Saturday, I was giving healing to my friend Jules when, to my surprise, a symbol appeared in my mind's eye and I clearly heard a voice telling me to look at page 57 in the book. I assumed this message was meant for her and quickly scribbled the symbol on a scrap of paper and handed her the book. Later, she contacted me and declared that neither resonated with her in any way but could she hold onto the book since it looked interesting. I felt a little disappointed but just accepted this and carried on with my busy life. When Jules returned the book, I stashed it on a shelf and ignored it ~ despite the fact that it fell from my bookcase right in front of me a grand total of three times!

Then, a year to the day later, Kate raced down from our healing room, excitedly announcing that she had been given a symbol. I then heard a voice say that I already had the Master symbol and had given it away! At this point I had no real understanding of what this meant, but trusted that I would. I did, however, have a feeling that this was of utmost importance. I frantically found and searched the book, shaking it vigorously but nothing fell out! So I meditated, asking for the symbol to be revealed to me again and, thankfully, it was. I also flicked through the pages until my eyes rested on page 57 and I experienced an astonishing feeling of peace.... of coming home.

The book was 'Jesus and the Essenes' by Dolores Cannon and page 57 depicted the Essene community of Qumran by the banks of The Dead Sea. At that moment, I knew without a shadow of doubt that I had lived there many life times before. I could smell and taste the salty air and feel the dry heat.

When the symbol appeared to me during this healing session it was accompanied by a past life experience, which replicated exactly in content and feeling one that I had visited previously. This experience occurred in the autumn of '03 when I had received an angel attunement and was schooled in the use of the Merkaba by Angela

McGerr. In the midst of the attunement I was transported to a desert landscape where I paced, numerous scrolls under my right arm, willing a nomadic friend to return from their travels with esoteric information. I felt a sense of urgency to receive and record this information, as if my life depended upon it!

I was feeling agitated and somewhat frustrated as my stomach churned with a massive surge of anticipation. Ultimately, after what seemed like an age, I perceived a dim, hazy figure on the horizon, which gradually took shape and began to resemble and be recognisable as my friend Jules, elatedly bringing obscure and wondrous information to me ~ information to be marvelled at then recorded. I felt that I was doing something massively important and secret, to be protected from all but a few privileged eyes.

At this point I had no idea of the meaning of this vision but knew the feelings were powerful and sensed that this was not the last I'd hear of it! I was right because these exact same images and feelings returned, as the symbol suddenly appeared that day. So far I had only experienced brief glimpses of this life, which ultimately to be fleshed out, to my amazement, in subsequent past life regressions.

Back to the day that Kate shared with me that she'd received a symbol ... I was 'told' the symbol I'd previously been given was called Nomada and, quite naturally, assumed that this referred to the nomadic wanderings necessary to find its essence, the esoteric wisdom associated with it. Both being Reiki Masters, we were used to working with the energy of symbols, so we immediately began to use it on ourselves and others, to develop a relationship with it, to breathe it into life. Gradually, we realised its enormity ~ its deliciously gentle yet all-pervading power.

As other symbols emerged, making a grand total of thirteen and eventually forming a complete healing system, we were able to use them in tandem with Nomada, to experience how its subtlety and mastery allowed their energies to flow. It facilitated their opening, their flowering and the sharing of their unique magic. As time passed we began to construct an understanding of this magnificent symbol, of what it meant and what it had to offer. It felt like the signature symbol of the new healing system, describing a journey through healing and enlightenment prompted by receiving and basking in its energy. A journey that involved an initial phase characterised by the frenetic activity of searching, yearning, striving followed by tearful, heartfelt relief at finally experiencing calm, peace, stillness. Ultimately, reaching the absolute serenity of arriving home ~ to a place of comfort and tranquillity, a place of peace and love. We came to appreciate that this final stage of joyous relief incorporates an understanding that all answers can be found within ourselves, where they've always resided and not outside in some external situation, individual or object.

We had arrived home!

For additional information about Dolores Cannon and her work access www.ozarkmt.com

You can find more information about Angela McGerr and her work at www.angelamcgerr.com

NOMADA ~ THE MASTER SYMBOL

- *Calm, stillness, peace following a period of searching/striving*
- *Coming home to truth/wisdom within*

This is the signature symbol, defining and describing the nature of the energy. The name, Nomada, may allude to the nomadic roaming and searching prior to realising, via esoteric knowledge and wisdom, the key to peace, serenity and harmony. Note: The numbers and arrows denote how I 'saw' it being drawn.

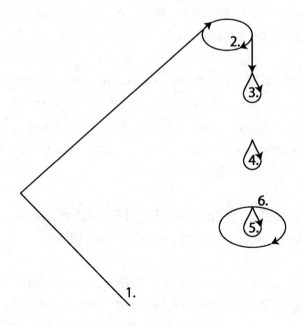

Using Nomada

- *To fill a room with calm, peace and tranquillity*

Take a few slow, deep breaths and feel your feet firmly on the ground. Using your preferred hand, draw the symbol Nomada in the air on every wall, then on the floor and ceiling. As you draw, repeat the mantra, "I fill this space with calm, peace and tranquillity".

Stand back and get a sense of the energy created, feel the peace in every part of your being, breathe it in, allow it to circulate around your body, to touch your mind.

Repeat whenever you have a sense that the room's energy is becoming contaminated again.

Expect to feel the peace and calm every time you enter the room. If it's a shared room, expect your interactions here to be more harmonious. Expect all those who share this space to be calmer and more peaceful. If it's a bedroom, expect to sleep better.

You can change the wording if you wish, for example, "I fill this space with love, serenity and bliss".

- *To feel empowered and fill yourself with love and light (best performed outside on a starlit night)*

Stand with legs hip width apart and place your hands on your solar plexus to centre yourself. Take three slow, deep breaths. Stretch your arms above your head, placing your forefingers and thumbs together making a triangle to frame the stars. Slowly draw their energy into your crown chakra and down to your third eye. Gradually draw the energy down to the solar plexus and rest your hands there, again taking slow, deep breaths.

Place your hands in the prayer position, visualise Nomada in silver/violet light and, chanting its name three times, move your hands upwards over the crown chakra and outwards in a semi-circle returning your hands to the prayer position.

Placing your hands on your heart, right hand over left, push palms downwards to your base chakra stating: "I fill my entire being with the healing love and light of the stars".

Repeat three times. Smile!

Alternatively, you may like to state: "I fill my entire being with peace, with calm, with stillness... I am home!"

HEALING WITH SYMBOLS

As you read about the following symbols I imagine you'll be keen to 'play' with them, to experiment with their energy and experience them working for you and any issues or problems you may have. I've included a few specific ways of using them under each chapter heading and here offer you some general guidelines that I hope will be useful.

You don't have to draw the symbols exactly as they are presented here. It's their essence that's important and your intention as you use them.

Feel free to use your intuition, placing the symbols wherever feels right for you and choosing whichever symbols call to you. The symbols have their own intelligence and their energy will automatically go wherever it's most needed to foster the highest good and greatest joy of the recipient.

When using symbols you can tap, clap or blow them in saying their name three times if you wish.

Remember to ground yourself or the other person carefully at the end of a healing session. You can do this using a specific symbol on the feet or simply by holding the feet and visualising them being connected to the Earth in some way. You can repeat the mantra, "Safe, supported, grounded".

Also, give thanks both at the beginning and end of a healing session to whichever beings you've been supported by e.g. God/Goddess, angels, spirit guides, etc.

Here are just a few ideas of how you can use the symbols. There are numerous other ways, please use your imagination. I have divided them up into self healing and healing others and, in both cases, have included a preliminary relaxation/invocation.

Self-healing

Find the most comfortable position you can, either lying or sitting with your back straight.

Begin by making sure you are grounded, that your feet are touching the ground or that you have grounded them by imagining roots growing from your soles deep into the core of Mother Earth, receiving her love, her nurturing, her strength and stability. You may use any other way that works for you.

Slow your breathing down by taking a few slow, deep breaths.

Allow your body to relax by dropping your shoulders, relaxing the muscles in your face, allowing your arms to fall gently in your lap or at your side. Feel yourself getting heavy, heavier and heavier and more and more relaxed. Repeat the mantra, "I am calm. I am relaxed. I am safe".

State your intention for the healing and thank your guides/helpers/spiritual beings for being with you and guiding, supporting and inspiring you throughout this process.

Say, "I open my heart centre and allow this healing experience in" and enjoy a sense of optimism as you embrace this positive experience.

Here's an invocation, written by a treasured member of our Anusha community, Lesley, which you may like to use or modify according to your specific needs.

Lesley's Anusha invocation
for self-healing

I call to my guides, angels and spirits that surround the star-bright energy of Anusha.

My heart is open and my faith is true as I feel the love and healing energy you send nourish my body and feed my soul.

I gratefully accept lessons to be learned and messages received that bring me closer to myself.

In love and peace and joy.

Thank you.

Now, proceed in any of the following ways:

Draw the symbol on each palm in turn using one or two fingers (forming a mudra) of the opposite hand, almost like drawing with a pen. Clap your hands together chanting the name of the symbol three times (to manifest the energy). This is often referred to as 'powering up' your hands. As always with energy work your intention is paramount and stating this clearly out loud or in your head acts as a trigger and positively manifests the outcome. Place your hands wherever you are intuitively guided.

Draw the symbol in front of you in your aura, which for most people is around 10–15 cm from their physical body, then visualise the symbol's energy filling your aura, remembering to allow it to flow under your feet, totally surrounding you, like being wrapped in a soft, comforting blanket.

Put the symbol directly into your body in a specific place, into a particular chakra, limb, muscle, organ, gland etc.

Draw the symbol on a piece of paper and place under your healing couch, bed or chair.

After the healing session ground yourself carefully.

At the end of the healing flick from your hands any excess energy or pass your hands over a candle flame or hold a cleansing crystal of your choice.

Again, thank your guides/helpers/spiritual beings for being present throughout your healing experience.

Healing others

Healing others can be done 'hands on' (that is, when you are physically in the same room as the recipient) and it can also be achieved from a distance. Often when we think of healing we imagine a particular person to send to, although we can send healing randomly to groups of people, for example people in the town where we live. Healing can be also be sent using a crystal grid or healing book.

Prepare a sacred space. State your intention for the healing and thank your guides/helpers/spiritual beings for being with you and guiding, supporting and inspiring you throughout this process.

Open your heart centre and allow love and healing energy to flow.

Lesley also wrote an invocation for healing others, which you may like to use or modify according to your specific needs.

Lesley's Anusha invocation for healing others

I call to my guides, angels and spirits that surround the star-bright energy of Anusha.

My heart is open and my intention is true as I feel the love and healing energy you send nourish the body and complete/feed the soul of ...

I gratefully accept lessons to be learned and messages received that bring us closer to ourselves.

In love and peace and joy.

Thank you.

Prepare yourself by drawing the symbol on each palm as before and then clap your hands together chanting the name of the symbol three times. If you wish, draw a particular symbol over all of your chakras or put a symbol into a specific chakra.

To give what is known as 'hands on' healing to an individual, lay your hands on the person (having first asked their permission to do so), or simply allow your hands to hover in their aura, moving them according to your own intuitive guidance. Use your breath to blow the symbols in or your eyes to visualise the symbols in specific places. You can draw the symbol on the roof of your mouth with your tongue then click your tongue three times on the roof of your mouth whilst silently chanting the symbol's name before blowing it in.

Draw the symbols directly over the person's body, focusing their energy into specific chakras, limbs, muscles, organs, glands etc.

Place a large symbol over the entire body.
After the treatment remember to ground the person carefully.

At the end of the healing remove any extra energy you may have picked up by either shaking your hands three times or passing your hands over a candle flame or holding a cleansing crystal of your choice.

Again, thank your guides/helpers/spiritual beings for being present throughout this healing experience.

Just to emphasise that working with these symbols is a highly individual, intuitive process. Please do whatever feels right for you, remembering to invite in and thank your guides and to ground yourself or the other person thoroughly.

STEMMING THE TIDE OF PAIN

HOGARTH

When Kate raced down the stairs, excited to receive a symbol, she had been healing a client with acute persistent pain in the coccyx. The client's life was severely restricted by this immobilising pain and she had tried absolutely everything over many years and nothing had worked. During the healing, Kate said she was feeling massive empathy for her client and her predicament and was thinking to herself, "If only I had a symbol specifically for agonising pain" when a symbol took shape in her mind's eye! She focused on channelling the healing power of the symbol, whilst feeling surprised but willing to go with the flow of events. I asked if she'd been given a name and she tentatively murmured 'Hogarth'. She was somewhat bewildered that all this had happened and neither of us quite knew what to make of it, including this strange name. However, we did feel very grateful and, well, just got on with our day!

Soon afterwards we were given an opportunity to test out the symbol personally. We were walking through a barred gate in the countryside and Kate dropped the large metal latch on her hand and was screaming in agony. I immediately used the symbol to give her healing. My hand went red hot and within moments the pain had dissipated. The symbol not only served to lessen the pain but also reduced the associated shock, leaving Kate pain-free, calm and relaxed. We were delighted to have a symbol at our disposal that had such an immediate and powerful effect.

Kate also reported that she felt grounded when receiving the symbol and, when we asked friends to experience it, they concurred. Over the next few days we used it often with considerable success. We started using the symbol on the soles of clients' feet during and after treatments to help the person feel safe, supported and grounded. We also used it in a focused way, beaming its healing power into a particular area, which was identified by the client or by sensations in our hands whilst healing. We were also using Nomada and tried them out in combination and the result was staggering. We began to realise how immensely powerful this energy was.

As for Kate's client, the pain did not immediately subside but over time the client was empowered to move out of an untenable situation to one which was pleasing to her. At this point the pain was released!

Although Kate heard the symbol's name very clearly we had no real idea of its significance until many months later. We felt we 'should' have something specific, maybe profound even, to share with everyone about its meaning and had reached an uneasy acceptance that perhaps we simply would not. Then, on the eve of the Anusha Presentation in late October (more about this later), we had settled down to watch T.V. and were flicking through the channels when a programme caught our eye. The programme featured William Hogarth, the British painter, printmaker and satirist, who lived between 1697 and 1764.

We watched the programme with excited interest and discovered that, through his graphic and immensely detailed depictions of 18th Century poverty-stricken London and its population (The Rake's Progress, The Harlot's Progress, Gin Lane), he highlighted the extreme plight and pain of the poor. His strong belief in the possibility of change and desire to ground the disadvantaged sections of the population with social and economic reforms seemed to really resonate with the symbol. We were delighted to have something meaningful to share!

HOGARTH

- *Alleviates physical pain*
- *Shock*
- *Grounding*

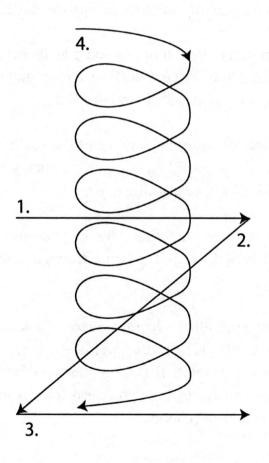

<u>Using Hogarth</u>

- *To anchor/ground yourself*

Stand or sit and take a few slow, deep breaths.

Look down and visualise Hogarth (in red light, if this feels right for you) encircling your feet and imagine its energy moving gently downwards into the Earth.

Repeat its name three times as you take its safe, steady energy down into the core of Gaea, connecting with the loving, nurturing energy of Mother Earth.

Imagine the loving, caring energy of the Earth merging with Hogarth's grounding, supportive energy and feel this combined force returning to you.

As the energy reaches the soles of your feet, feel it becoming magnified and pouring through your entire body.

Feel this grounding, loving energy touching and caressing every part of you: every cell, every muscle, every sinew ~ running like warm marrow through your bones. Take whatever time you need to fill your being with this stabilising energy.

When you feel ready, take a few slow, deep breaths and return. Take a moment to give thanks.

- *To ground another whilst giving healing*

At an appropriate time, as guided, 'draw' Hogarth on the soles of the person's feet, tapping in the energy three times as you repeat its name. You can do this on each foot in turn or together.

Visualise the person being connected through the symbol to the majestic love and nurture of Mother Earth.

If you wish, repeat the mantra, "Safe, supported, grounded ... safe, supported, grounded ... safe, supported, grounded".

As always, thank your guides and the spiritual beings around you for their loving support.

- *To minimise pain/shock*

Direct the healing energy of Hogarth into a specific place/area of the person's body whilst visualising the person being fully functioning, pain-free, grounded and healed.

Ask for information to be revealed to the person about the source of the pain or reason for the shock and, perhaps, its meaning and significance for them. Ask that they receive this in a way that feels positive and empowering for them. Express your gratitude.

BALANCING LIGHT & DARK

TABOR

A few days later Kate emerged from the healing room, sporting a wide grin, saying that another symbol had come through. The client she was working with this time had crippling arthritis and high blood pressure, and, again, she'd thought, "Wouldn't it be nice if I had a specific symbol for this". As usual, she was spending a good deal of time at the person's head with her eyes closed and instantly saw the symbol "written in the air". She heard the word 'Tabor' and saw the symbol very clearly. She was immediately able to draw it for me and described precisely the order and direction she saw it being drawn in. We had no notion of what 'Tabor' meant but just accepted it, in the same way that we had accepted the name of the previous symbol. We still hadn't realised that a complete energy healing system was being revealed to us and were being rather vague and somewhat scatty about the whole thing!

Again, we worked on ourselves with the symbol's energy and, comparing notes, agreed that it also had the ability to achieve balance ~ balancing conflicting energies, balancing opposing forces, balancing light and dark energy. Using the symbol on friends and clients supported this idea ~ if a person, for example, was struggling with difficulties, feeling bleak and low and had temporarily lost a connection with anything positive in their life, then Tabor would help in restoring a sense of balance and open them up for their optimism to flow. We discovered that when people experienced an imbalance between their head and heart, either remaining entirely logical about something or overwhelmingly emotional, then Tabor's energy would serve to blend aspects of both, bringing the client into harmonic balance.

Sometime later, Kate googled the word 'Tabor' and was surprised to discover that Mount Tabor is a dome-shaped mountain six miles east of Nazareth in Israel. It is the very mountain on which Jesus appeared to Peter, James and John on Easter Saturday between his crucifixion and ascension. She read that Jesus appeared transfigured, his face shone like the sun, and he became as white as the light. The picture shown of Jesus, holding out his arms and being bathed in pure white light streaming down from above, moved us and reminded us, uncannily, of the appearance of the symbol and its transformative energy.

TABOR

- *Arthritis*
- *Blood pressure*
- *Balancing light/dark energies*

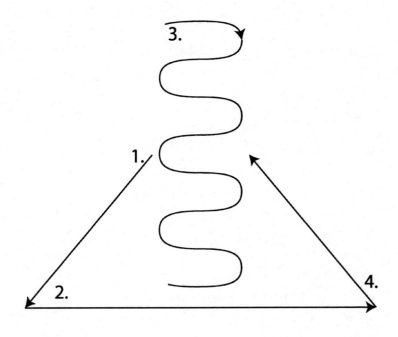

Using Tabor

- *To achieve balance*

Surround a situation or person with the energy of Tabor to bring about balance. Either visualise or actually 'draw' the symbol encircling the person/problem to be healed whilst tapping and intoning its name three times. Give thanks for the healing.

- *To minimise the pain of arthritis*

Focus Tabor's energy on a particular area affected by arthritis and visualise either an apex (whichever one feels right to you) or the bottom of its 'snake' pointing towards this area, again tapping and intoning its name three times. Express your gratitude for the healing.

- *To lower or raise blood pressure*

Focus Tabor's energy over the recipient's heart chakra and tap whilst intoning its name three times. Give thanks.

PUTTING BOUNDARIES IN PLACE

KANUE

By this time we began to realise that something pretty special was happening and that perhaps we were being given a series of symbols that constituted some kind of healing system. We started to use them much more consciously, more extensively, and then we would share our experiences, always holding a boundary around the client's confidentiality. We posed a torrent of questions, like, "How did it feel to use the symbol?", "What did you pick up from the person?", "How did you use it?", "Where did you put it?", "How did you put it in?", "What feedback did you get?", "What else did you see, hear, feel, experience?". We were beginning to use the symbols together and gradually get a feel for the potential of their energies and how they could be synthesised into a healing system.

Then, Kate scored a hat trick! Kate was working with Jules F, who had some psoriasis on his knees and elbows, which had caused him aggravation for considerable time. Again she thought, "Oh, I really wish I had a symbol", and she later told me that, at that exact moment, "it just popped in!". The symbol worked brilliantly! Much to the client's delight the psoriasis had virtually disappeared within two or three weeks, after just a few sessions. Kate described it as, "one of the most miraculous healings I've ever done". We began using it with clients and hearing from them the enormously positive effects it was having. We soon realised that it was a really strong symbol and, that, although Kate had brought it in to work with skin disorders, its effects were far reaching. Whilst discussing its healing potential, we had a Eureka moment! We made the connection that ultimately it was about boundaries. The skin is the boundary of the body; it's what keeps the body separate from the rest of the environment, it's what enables the body to feel safe, contained ~ a coherent whole organism. Kanue could be used to either strengthen boundaries or loosen them, whichever was appropriate and most helpful for the person.

This process of realisation was extremely organic, much the same as it had been with all the symbols. We needed to go through this experiential process before we engaged our logical minds and realised its wider use.

Googling the word Kanue later we discovered that Kanyu (which basically sounds the same and Kate only hears an approximate sound as a general rule) means to study the flow of energy chi, how to contain it in the right spot and harvest its positive benefits. If you cast your eye on the form of this symbol, you'll see how appropriate this is!

KANUE

- *Skin eruptions*
- *Strengthening boundaries*
- *Emerging from hiding*

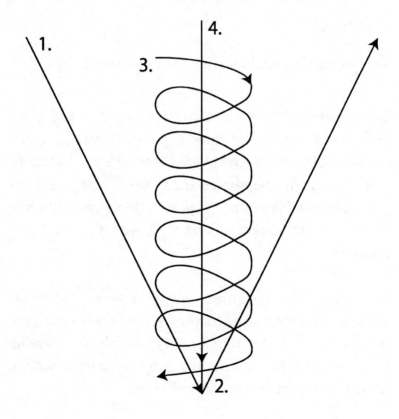

<u>Using Kanue</u>

Kanue like all the other symbols has its own intelligence and will work in whatever way is necessary to promote the person's highest good and greatest joy. Consequently, as a healer you do not necessarily need to know whether the recipient needs to firm up their boundaries or relax them to engage in healthy interaction with others, Kanue will do whatever is appropriate.

- *To establish healthy boundaries around yourself*

Sit quietly, taking a few slow, deep breaths and place your hands over your solar plexus. Gently pose the question of yourself, "What area of my life would benefit from a shift in boundaries right now?" and just allow your inner wisdom to respond. Don't question the response, just accept and let it sit with you for a few moments.

Now, taking another three slow, deep breaths visualise the symbol surrounding that issue, situation or even the person or people involved. You may simply allow Kanue to settle within your aura, easing its energy into a particular chakra or area of your body.

Now in as much detail as possible visualise the boundaries shifting, how you will feel when they have, how others will respond to you, how you will be around others. Bring in all your senses ... see, hear, feel, smell, taste ... and allow yourself to experience these amazing improvements.

Take whatever time you need to fully immerse yourself in these changes, then assert, "My boundaries are perfect ... everything and everyone are in their right place".

- *To establish healthy boundaries around others*

When working with clients you can go through the same process, connecting to their higher consciousness and bathing them in Kanue's energy. You can pour it through your hands (having powered them up first by 'clapping in' the symbol), or apply the symbol directly to a particular area, using its apex to focus the energy ~ or blow it in with your breath.

- *To power yourself up the Lesley way**

Stand with feet hip width apart and take a few slow, deep breaths to steady yourself. Now, draw Kanue in line with your body by starting the 'V' shape to your left above your left shoulder, then bringing the apex down to the ground between your feet and completing the 'V' back up to your right side above your right shoulder. Then begin tracing the spiral down the centre of the 'V' in line with your seven charkas and finish with a strong downwards sweep right through the spiral, anchoring the symbol into the ground. If you're left handed draw the 'V' in the opposite direction.

With love and thanks to Lesley for this imaginative idea.

- *Using Tabor and Kanue together*

Tabor and Kanue complement each other very well and, when used together, can balance light and dark energies so setting protective boundaries firmly and appropriately in place.

Travelling Back to Move Forwards

Past Life Regression

Around this time I felt strongly that these symbols and their underlying energy was extremely familiar, that we were being reminded about them rather than actually discovering them for the first time. I decided to access a past life regression with the express purpose of asking the questions, "Where did this healing energy come from?", "When were we given it originally?" and "Who gave it to us?".

Our close friend, Frankie, is a hypnotherapist who specialises in, amongst other things, Past Life Regression. She was delighted to conduct the sessions and, with open minds and hearts and in excited anticipation, we went ahead. We had a series of two regressions and the second was particularly illuminating.

The script of this regression follows. To set the scene, having taken me into a hypnotic trance, Frankie (in italics) asked me to look around and tell her where I was:

Looks like a desert.

Look down at your feet - what are you wearing on your feet? They're little brown feet, naked.

How old are you? I'm 3 – 4 years old, scrawny.

Boy or girl? A boy.

What is your name? Jacob – Isaiah.

Do you know what year it is? Adults will know.

1, 2, 3 moving on: I'm bigger, stronger now – a powerful man. They call me Jacob the Protector. Living in changing times – great upheaval all around me. The Messiah is here.

Do you know him well? He is a friend, a mentor.

What is happening now? Feels like several years – no one really knows, momentous times – time of confusion and upheaval. Just to know I am living in important times.

Where in the world are you?   Damascus. Quite bleak here. See, but have no blackness inside.

How do you spend your days?   A very simple man – I protect lepers from people who want to kill them. I do simple tasks – some would say beneath a man. I fetch water and food. Quite isolated here. I perform some of the tasks generally done by womankind.

1, 2, 3 moving on: I'm much older, very, very frail. Feels like many years have passed but I know they haven't. Each year seems like ten – they have taken their toll on my body. Now very feeble.

How old are you now?   28 years old – feeling so, so old.

What is significant about this time for you?   This is the year that the Messiah comes to me and helps me to pass from this feeble body – helps me to move over knowing that I have done my life's work. He places his hands on my head – completely at peace. Says I have fulfilled every expectation – been a good man – can go in peace.

How do you die?   I slip away joyfully, peacefully.

Would you have done anything differently?   No.

What knowledge would you like to bring back with you? To help others. To serve others is the greatest gift I can give myself.   Peace.

This life was immensely vivid. I had a strong sense of my simplicity, my goodness, and my dedication to others. I also felt exhausted beyond my years and feeble, quite frail. I could feel the healing energy from the Messiah pouring into my crown and a sense of absolute bliss pervading my whole being. I knew I'd lived an honourable life and the satisfaction of that knowledge was particularly important to me.

Afterwards I meditated on the experience of being Jacob and knew that I was Jacob the Essene. I also intuitively felt that the healing I received from Jesus had the same loving, forgiving and compassionate feel to it as the healing energy that we were currently being given. I was amazed and delighted by this realisation. Sharing this with Kate later stirred a memory for her of receiving a stunning attunement to Sekhem energy from a luminous and lovely woman, Leela. During this deeply metaphysical and hypnotic attunement, Leela channelled that Kate had been very close to Jesus, part of his inner circle. Everything was falling into place . . the book, the visions of the scrolls, Mount Tabor, the Essenes ... Jesus.

Frances (Frankie) Free is a counsellor and hypnotherapist specialising in past life regression therapy who regularly makes use of the symbols in her work in this field. Contact her via www.hypnotherapyhighwycombe.co.uk

LeelaLight says, "My passion and love is helping others into Living in their Light and their Self-Expression here on Earth, thereby bringing light, joy and love to themselves and their world in glorious reflection." Contact her at www.loveandinsight.com

REVISITING QUMRAN

The feeling of coming home when I glanced at the picture of Qumran filled me with comfort, a reassuring warmth. I just knew that I'd lived there, even though I'd never visited in this lifetime. Hearing from Leela that Kate had known Jesus and experiencing his closeness in my regression confirmed to us that we had been part of a community that he frequented. Although, as Jacob, I was living in Damascus, I was to discover in later regressions at least one other life spent in Qumran.

I resolved to find out more about the Essenes and was pleasantly surprised to find a wealth of written material. Although little had been known about them beforehand, considerable information had been gleaned from the Dead Sea Scrolls, accidentally discovered from 1947 onwards in the caves of Qumran and other locations near the Dead Sea. Edmond Bordeaux Szekely has written prolifically about the Essenes and translated many texts from the Scrolls. Additionally, information about them and their way of life was channelled in fascinating past life regressions, reported by Dolores Cannon in the superb 'Jesus and the Essenes', the very book that had first drawn my attention to this community. Surprisingly, I didn't actually read this book until after my regression! Another invaluable source of information for me, again based on regression material, was the excellent book by Stuart Wilson and Joanna Prentis, 'The Essenes: Children of the Light'. I present here merely the briefest sketch of my understanding.

It is believed that the Essene brotherhood lived for around three hundred years spanning Jesus' birth, mainly in towns and villages near the Dead Sea in Israel. Their numbers included men, women and children and the communities were diverse in that priests, lay people, craftsmen, teachers, astronomers, farmers etc. all co-existed. They practiced a communal way of life, sharing everything equally, having great respect for each other and the natural world and dedicating themselves to an existence of peace and harmony. They engaged in healing on a regular basis and poured creative love into every aspect of their lives, their work, their relationships, and all their activities.

The Essenes were predominantly vegetarian and practiced an extensive knowledge of agriculture, which enabled them to grow a wide variety of vegetables and fruits. They lived very simply, rising early, bathing in cold water and wearing white garments. In the morning they studied and connected with the natural world; they worked hard all day, either in the fields or at other productive activities, and in the evenings they studied and connected with angels, a different angel on each day of the week. Their lifestyle meant they were immensely healthy, often living up to 120 years.

The Brotherhood studied education, healing, astronomy and ancient writings. Indeed, it has been suggested that the fact they studied widely and were influenced by a broad system of thought may have presented a challenge to orthodox Jews, who perhaps perceived them as subversive. This may explain the Essene tendency towards secrecy; they were very protective of themselves and their way of life.

They lived according to the 'One Law', passed down by Moses. Moses discovered that every living and non-living thing was governed by the same universal law. 'The Law' governs all that takes place in the universe, it creates life and it creates thought. All manner of things, including every individual, form a dynamic unity according to 'the Law'.

The abstract idea of 'the Law' was conveyed by the symbol of a tree called The Tree of Life, symbolising that man was a unity of energy, thoughts and emotions and, as a unit of life force, was constantly communing with the totality of energies in the universe. The roots of the Tree of Life represent seven earthly forces, namely the Earthly Mother, the angels of Earth, Life, Joy, the Sun, Water and Air. The branches represent seven cosmic forces, the Heavenly Father, and his angels of Eternal Life, Creative Work, Peace, Power, Love and Wisdom. Man exists in the centre of the tree surrounded by all the forces; the Essenes lived their life in contact and harmony with these forces through morning and evening communions and noon contemplations. Indeed, they only recognised positive and constructive forces in the Universe.

Jesus was one of many healers and teachers, alongside John the Baptist sent out by the Brotherhood. They were dedicated to spreading their concept of sevenfold peace: peace with the body; the mind; with the family; with humanity; with culture and, finally, with the Kingdom of the Earthly Mother and the Heavenly Father. The community provided an extensive support structure for Jesus, an integrated spiritual family.

As I read through this fascinating information I resonated with it at a soul level, especially the concepts of egalitarian living and the emphasis on inner peace and harmony rather than external gratification and material wealth.

WHAT'S IN A NAME?

ANUSHA

I was talking with a dear and valued friend about life purpose, what we're here to achieve and how it shapes our lives. I'd shared that I believed I was here this time round to disseminate information that would help people cope with, and rise in a constructive way to, the challenges presented by the immense changes happening here on earth, particularly with 2012 on the horizon. Information that would facilitate healing; right across the spectrum from individuals healing themselves to group healing for the planet. Having received the Master symbol a year before and, only realising its significance when Hogarth, Tabor and Kanue came through that same month, I was buzzing with enthusiasm and heightened emotion. I felt that I was destined to share this healing energy in some special way, yet at that time had a hunch that there was more to come; we only had a few pieces of the jigsaw. I remember describing, in quite an animated way, the experience of realising that we were being given something pretty huge and groping to find the words to do it all justice. In these moments of excitement and frustration, I realised that the energy didn't yet have a name!

When I beamed into my friend's energy, I had a graphic and detailed vision of him as a monk, a Franciscan. This was accompanied by a sense of loving, unconditional and totally selfless service. I told my friend this and he nodded in recognition, saying he felt strongly that, in this life, his mission was to love unconditionally, with an exquisite purity; that he was not expecting to receive anything for himself at all. I was extremely moved and touched by this selflessness and felt tears prick the back of my eyes. As I left to return home, I retained this vivid feeling of profound love in my heart. Love that transforms, that heals, that knows or recognises no bounds. Love that focuses our attention on what's important ~ the heart-to-heart and soul-to-soul connection between others and ourselves.

I drifted into a reverie as I drove, then heard, as a whisper at first, then becoming louder and louder, a word that sounded like 'Aneesha' or 'Anisha' or 'Anusha'. I experienced a frisson of excitement and felt sure that the name of the healing energy was being given to me. I raced indoors as soon as I arrived home and scratched the words hurriedly on a scrap of paper. I kept repeating them to myself, allowing them to roll around on my tongue, and then explode from my mouth as I said them out loud. I decided to google them but initially felt no real resonance with any of the possible meanings I'd uncovered.

Light faded into dusk as I eventually let out a gasp ~ I'd found it! I'd discovered that Anusha is the name of a star in Hindu astronomy and also means, 'beautiful morning, the first rays of light at dawn' in Hindi. I pictured an image of shimmering light rising and sparkling on dew with the promise of a glorious new day after the darkness of night, after the beaming stars had poured their lustrous energy over the Earth. I knew this was right. I just knew Anusha was the name of the healing energy!

DEFINITELY NOT ALONE!

ANGELS & ASCENDED MASTERS

When we were giving healing we had the sense that we being supported or accompanied by spiritual beings. Often clients reported that they felt several sets of hands on their bodies and sometimes opened an eye to peep and check out what was happening! One particularly sensitive soul remarked that she 'saw' a whole queue of beings lining up behind me with their hands resting on my shoulders and beaming their combined healing energy through me to her. Another 'saw' a translucent white angel with beautiful unfurled wings hovering over her entire body for the duration of the healing session. Many reported sensing energies in the room before, during and after healing. Over the years I had had several astonishing experiences with angels and knew they were beside me keeping me safe, supporting and inspiring me. They often communicated messages to me and to the clients I worked with. I usually know when there are angels present because I sneeze rather loudly, once for each angel!

I decided to take myself into a meditation to talk to these angels and ask for more information about them. I was told that the angels alongside us for Anusha were Camael, Zadkiel and Cassiel. I hurriedly consulted 'A Harmony of Angels' by Angela McGerr and other sources of esoteric information. Although angels are androgynous, I tend to characterise them in my mind as either male or female depending on how I experience their energies. I perceive both Camael and Cassiel as female and Zadkiel as male.

I discovered that Camael's name means 'She who sees God' and that she is particularly associated with the qualities of courage, empowerment and justice. Camael is the angel of the third ray, Chief of the powers, ruler of Mars and the fifth heaven. Her crystals include ruby, garnet, red agate and carnelian. Her temple is located in St. Louis, USA.

My various sources revealed that Zadkiel means 'Righteousness of God' and that he is the angel of the seventh ray, Chief of the order of dominions, ruler of Jupiter and the sixth heaven. His crystals are lapis lazuli and turquoise and he is associated with abundance, wisdom and success. Zadkiel's temple is located in Cuba.

Cassiel, the angel associated with peace, harmony and serenity, whose name means 'Speed of God' is Chief of the order of Cherubim, ruler of Saturn and the seventh heaven. Her crystals are obsidian, onyx, rutilated quartz and black agate.

Working with the Angels

Each of these extraordinary beings has different energy and, although fairly subtle, they can usually be differentiated from each other. There are myriad ways of calling in the angels and we all feel them slightly differently, perhaps a gentle caress on the back of a hand, a warm sensation in our heart, a light breeze blowing, finding a wispy white feather. I prefer to simply say the angel's name three times and invite them with pure unconditional love to bring their special qualities into my life or to work on a specific issue.

Here's an invocation to use to draw in the combined healing energy of these Anusha Angels:

"Cassiel, Zadkiel, Camael ... shimmering and glorious beings of pure love and light, I welcome you with profound and unconditional love to help me connect with my inner harmony and serenity ... to resonate with my inner wisdom and power ... to feel calm and at peace ... to be at one ... In love and light, love and light, love and light ... Thank you angels, Thank you Divine Source."

We also felt that certain Ascended Masters were working with and through us, channelling information as well as the symbols. An Ascended Master is a soul who, after many incarnations and experiences, has learnt the lessons of the earthly realm and is able to ascend to a higher level of consciousness, a higher vibrational frequency. They then have the option to serve planet Earth in its ascension process as mass consciousness evolves. Ascended Masters communicate or channel to us through meditations, dreams, synchronicities, art, music and other expressions of the creative mind. Connecting with an Ascended Master enables us to access and activate higher knowledge, a knowledge that is inherently ours and already resides within us.

We had confirmation from the Past Life Regression that the primary source of inspiration for us was the Ascended Master Sananda (known as Jesus or The Messiah in his earthly incarnation). From my meditations, I discovered that the Masters Kuthumi and St. Germain were also supporting him.

My usual foray into exploration unearthed the following information. Esoteric traditions view that Sananda serves as World Teacher and is renowned as one of the greatest spiritual healers and teachers ever to incarnate on Earth.

Kuthumi is generally regarded as the conveyer of knowledge, wisdom and understanding in times of change. He comes to those who seek knowledge and fosters a desire to use that accumulated knowledge for the good of all. He serves with Sananda as World Teacher.

It is generally believed that Kuthumi had many incarnations, which included Pythagoras, the Greek philosopher and mathematician. He travelled widely in his quest for truth, exchanging information and ideas with priests and scholars. He was tutored by the Magi in music, astronomy, and the sacred science of invocation and founded a mystery school of the Great White Brotherhood in Southern Italy. Here he gathered together carefully selected men and women and together they pursued a philosophy based upon the mathematical expression of universal law. He believed that number is both the form and the essence of creation.

Another of Kuthumi's incarnations was as Balthazar, one of the three Wise Men, who followed the star to the child, Jesus. He brought the treasure of his realm, frankincense, as a gift to Christ.

Kuthumi was also said to have incarnated as St. Francis of Assisi, who gave up his considerable wealth to live a life of poverty among the poor and the lepers. He found absolute joy in replicating the compassion of Christ and dedicated his life to praying peace, converting many disciples. People of all faiths throughout the world speak his prayer:

Lord, make me an instrument of peace
Where there is hatred, let me sow love
Where there is injury, let me sow pardon
Where there is error, let me sow truth
Where there is doubt, let me sow faith
Where there is despair, let me sow hope
Where there is discord, let me sow unity
Where there is sadness, let me sow joy
Where there is darkness, let me sow light

Divine Master, grant that I might not so much seek
to be consoled, as to console
To be understood, as to understand
To be loved, as to love
For it is in giving that we receive
It is in pardoning that we are pardoned
And it is in dying of this ego and recognising the Christ
consciousness within us
That we are born to eternal life

The third Ascended Master, St. Germain is often referred to as the master alchemist. He is reputed to have been able to turn base metals into gold. This is perhaps a metaphor for the process of transformation or manifestation, turning something less valuable into something precious. He was known as the man who never dies and was reputed to have lived for over 350 years, staging his death between lifetimes. He was very wealthy, but no one knew how he had accumulated his great fortune. He was also an accomplished painter and musician and possessed an extensive knowledge of herbalism. St. Germain is said to have granted us the invaluable gift of The Violet Flame ~ more about this later.

Invoking the energy of Ascended Masters

"Welcome Sananda, Master Jesus, supreme spiritual teacher, healer and visionary. Welcome Kuthumi, conveyer of knowledge, wisdom and understanding in these times of change. Welcome St. Germain, alchemist and magical transformer. Thank you, Ascended Masters, for supporting, guiding and inspiring us as we prepare to connect with ourselves, each other and to the Divine Source."

SEEING STARS!

THE SIX-POINTED STAR

We just kept seeing stars whilst we were giving healing and they were always six-sided. We believed this must be significant so did our usual googling act and discovered that the six-pointed star has many different meanings and interpretations depending on which religious or spiritual tradition it features in.

We were particularly drawn to the notion that the triangle pointing upwards symbolises good deeds flowing upwards to heaven, which then activates a corresponding flow of goodness back to the world, represented by the downward pointing triangle. This resonates with the mirroring idea of 'as above, so below'.

The star, as you probably know, is often referred to as The Star of David (after King David) and may be a representation of the configuration of planets at the time of his birth or when he became King and/or a symbol depicted on his magical shield, which protected him from his enemies.

We read with interest that the symbol could have been derived from the Knights Templars, an order instituted in AD1113 to protect pilgrims on their journey from Europe to the Holy Land. Kate has always been drawn to the Knights Templars, having experienced a glimpse of a past life where she was battling for the Templar cause.

Eastern religions perceive the two triangles to be in harmonious embrace, the downward triangle symbolising Shakti and the upward Shiva and their mystical union representing creation. Shiva is the Hindu Lord of Creation, paradoxically the ultimate destroyer of the world prior to its re-creation. He is responsible for change, both in the form of death and destruction and in terms of shedding old habits. Shakti is the Hindu Mother Goddess, the universal principle of energy, power and creativity. She represents the divine force, manifesting to destroy demonic forces and restore perfect balance.

This Eastern interpretation really appeals to me. I can feel in my heart the energetic pulsing of Shiva, sometimes known as The Lord of the Dance, and the creative power of his union with the balancing, vibrant energy of Shakti. Both immensely powerful ~ an embrace of equals. Anusha feels to me to encapsulate the notion of equality; of male and female energy, of mind, body and spirit, of desire with desired!

FILLING THE VOID

ANJA

The best way to share how this symbol came through is to relay Kate's own words, whilst we were both in conversation with our dear friend, Suse in preparation for writing this book:

"I was working with a client with whom I'd been working for some considerable time, someone I'd actually shared past lives with. I discovered in a past life regression with Frankie that I'd cut her throat in a previous life. Of course, she never knew that; I never told her. It was when I was guarding Jesus' family after his death. I was part of a group who were moving them to a place of safety. It was a caravan, I think, there were a series of tents, and they always had to be hidden so the servants couldn't see them. I was having a relationship with this particular servant girl and the curtains just happened to blow open and she caught a glimpse of the family. I had to immediately cut her throat, which was horrible, really, really horrible, but I had to. At the time I remember I didn't want to do it but I had no choice and I just did it, just in an instant. I feel really emotional talking about it now".

Kate went on to explain that, "this particular client has MS and an eating disorder and there was a huge hopelessness about her. I was feeling quite hopeless when I was giving her healing and I just really wanted a symbol to help her. So, this symbol came through very clearly, boom ... and it was there and I heard a word that sounded like 'Anja'. As it came through, I knew it was for hopelessness, MS and eating disorders. I'm aware that there can be a link between eating disorders and MS. I believe that an appropriate diet, a really good oily fish diet, can alleviate the symptoms of MS by helping to repair the myelin sheaths of the nerves. Anyway, she came for a long time and made improvements".

Suse wondered about the symbol resembling an eye and a tear and we speculated about the fact that the client, as the servant girl, had seen what she shouldn't have seen and she cried tears of sadness, or the drop could be blood dripping from her throat ~ it all felt connected somehow.

As we continued to work with the symbol and explore its potential we realised that it also had a favourable effect on many energy depleting conditions such as ME and Depression.

When Kate googled Anja she found and resonated with the following information. Aanjar, which sounded the same as the word she heard, is an archaeological site 58 km from Beirut in the Lebanon. It is unique in that, whereas other historical sites feature different civilisations superimposed on each other, Aanjar is exclusively one period ~ the Umayyad. It dates back to the early 8th century AD and only flourished for a few decades. The Umayyads are credited with the great Arab conquests that created an extensive Islamic empire. They were defeated when their rivals took advantage of their increasing decadence. Again, we could equate this with the symbol, the arching eyebrow representing the conquests, the over-seeing eye, the tear of defeat. The notion of expending huge amounts of energy in conquest and celebration, then ultimately becoming defeated by human lusty desires ~ desperate, hopeless and lost!

ANJA

- *Hopelessness*
- *Eating disorders*
- *MS*
- *ME*
- *Depression*

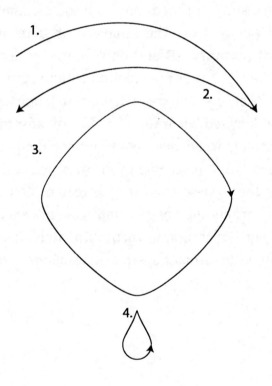

<u>Using Anja</u>

- *To lift you out of a stuck, hopeless place*

If you feel yourself in a depressed or hopeless state then visualise the symbol in golden light above your head, swirling and spinning inside a bell jar, swirling to the point of melting, like translucent melted butter. Then visualise the bell jar tipping and the golden liquid filling your aura, your being. As it pours over you, open your chakras and allow them to absorb this healing golden energy. Feel a lifting of the negative thoughts and feelings that had previously invaded you. Stay with this feeling, absorbing the golden liquid healing until every last vestige of hopelessness has completely left you. Give thanks for this resulting light, optimistic feeling.

- *To protect you when venturing into challenging situations or encountering negative people*

When going into a challenging situation, which you have previously experienced as emotionally draining or about to interact with somebody really negative, draw the symbol over your heart beforehand to protect you and stop your energy from being sapped.

UNCONDITIONAL LOVE

ANSHAR

Anshar was revealed to Kate whilst she was working with a client who had asthma. She only saw this person a few times but knew instantly that what she really needed was unconditional love. Kate said that her client described never having been loved unconditionally and wondered if that hampered her ability to breathe in life. This made total sense in that conditions affecting the lungs could well be linked to the heart chakra and how much love a person has experienced in their life. Kate saw the symbol and heard its name very clearly and knew it needed to be placed squarely over the heart chakra. Afterwards, as we were working on ourselves and other clients we received the information that cancer would also benefit from the loving energy of Anshar and were reminded of studies we'd read about linking the incidence of cancer with traumatic experiences, particularly the acute pain and sadness of loss and bereavement. Anshar, then, was our symbol for pouring love, unconditional and profound love into the heart centre.

And the name of this lovingly powerful symbol?

Kate unveiled the information that Anshar was a Babylonian God associated with the heaven and sky as a whole and creator of Anu, a sky God of the 3rd heaven able to turn anything he said into a reality. This mirrored the extraordinary power of unconditional love; it can manifest all good in our lives!

ANSHAR

- *Unconditional love*
- *Asthma*
- *Cancer*

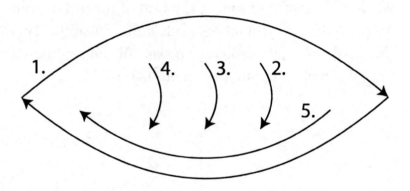

<u>Using Anshar</u>

- *To pour love into yourself or another*

Simply draw the symbol over your heart or the heart chakra of the other person and visualise it sinking in. Feel/see it going deeper and deeper, more and more penetrating. Visualise pure love pouring into the heart, filling it to the brim and overflowing outwards to every organ of the body until the entire body is full of exquisite love.

- *To ease the pain of cancer*

Place the symbol specifically in the area and visualise the tumour shrinking.

- *To ease asthma*

Place the symbol directly over the lungs. It can also be used to fill a room, car, etc. so the air becomes easier to breathe. Also, place an inhaler on a picture of the symbol or draw over the inhaler.

- *To ease conflict*

If you are venturing into or observing a conflict situation, visualise the symbol surrounding and merging with the people involved.

- *To 'soften' other symbols*

Use in combination with other symbols to allow the recipient to open up to receive the stronger, more challenging energies, for example with Anja.

NB. In this respect Anshar comes into its own with the increasingly powerful symbols, which come through later ~ more to follow.

BEING FIRED UP!

THE SILVER/VIOLET FLAME OF TRANSMUTATION

By this time we were both reporting having powerful and extraordinary experiences when healing ourselves and giving healing to others. Aches and pains were easing away and we both felt a sense of blissful satisfaction as we nestled into the loving, supportive energy of Anusha. We felt infinitely more loving towards others and accepting of ourselves. One day, whilst discussing what we experienced during healing sessions we realised that we were seeing massive amounts of silver and violet ~ interwoven, spiralling together, merging and dancing with each other in harmony. This struck us as significant and, although we appreciated each colour and its possible meaning, we decided to explore the implications of the two together being present so often when working with Anusha. Research revealed that there was a phenomenon called

The Silver Violet Flame of Grace and Transmutation. Evidently, the Violet Flame of Transmutation was gifted to humanity by the Divine Source in response to a request from the Ascended Master St. Germain following the massive surge of energy created by group prayer and meditation at the Harmonic Convergence.

This occurred in August of 1987 when there was an exceptional planetary alignment in the solar system, involving 8 planets being aligned in a 'grand trine'. This astonishing convergence was purported to correspond to an immense shift in energy towards a new age of peace and co-operation. The timing was said to coincide with the end of the 22 cycles each of 52 years (1144 years in total) described by the Mayan calendar, beginning the 26-year countdown to 2012. A time which many commentators predict as bringing an end to war, materialism, violence, abuse, injustice and oppression.

I was informed that, more recently, the Silver Ray of Grace and Harmony had merged with the Violet Flame to create the Silver Violet Flame of Grace and Transmutation. Over time the energetic vibration has expanded to encompass a wider range of colours, from pale lilac to deep violet. This flame is said to dissolve negative vibrations, so it can be used to transmute any emotion that feels negative ~ anger, judgement, jealousy, resentment etc. The flame can also purify relationships or past events, even from previous incarnations. To do this, simply visualise violet and silver flames surrounding whatever you want to purify. You can also call upon the flame to psychically cleanse your day by blazing a path ahead of you or to release a feeling of being stuck by inviting it into your body where you hold physical blocks. I was very moved when I read that the flame has this tremendous and impressive power to release and heal, that it helps us live in a loving place of power rather than a fearful place of powerlessness. We had our explanation of why we kept seeing this beautiful combination of colours and another invaluable tool for healing! (Editor's note: Not 2 years on from '87 the Berlin wall came down ...).

Using the Silver Violet Flame

Frankie wrote the following visualisation using the healing energy of the flame:

Place your feet on the ground ... rest your hands gently in your lap ... close your eyes ... take a few slow, deep breaths ... be at peace with yourself and the world around you ... as you embark on a wonderful voyage of healing and enlightenment.

Now ... place or sense your hands on your solar plexus ... as you do so, visualise a violet light shining down on you ... notice how the violet light shimmers and sparkles ... it is shot through with hundreds of silver flecks ... this is the Silver Violet Flame of Grace and Transmutation ...

It is as though this silver violet flame is being beamed to you from the stars ... notice how pale lilac and mauve seem to dance in the flame ... visualise these amazing colours – surrounding you, holding you, supporting you ... and, as you feel yourselves surrounded by the silver violet flame ...

Let go of any negative feelings that continue to bind you to events or relationships from the past ... let anger dissolve ... let go of fear ... allow the flame to blaze through your body purifying you ... healing you ...

Now imagine the beauty that is the silver violet flame surrounding someone you care for ... maybe someone you know who is struggling with events in their life at the moment ... send the silver violet flame to them ...

Now imagine the silver violet flame surrounding the whole planet ... cleansing it of negativity and beaming positive energy to all corners of the Earth ...

Affirm to yourself ... I am the silver violet flame, I am the silver violet flame, I am the silver violet flame, I hold the wisdom within ...

Breathe slowly and deeply ... feeling calm, serene, feeling relaxed and totally energised ... now, in your own time, coming slowly back ... open your eyes.

THE PERFECT NUMBER

THE NUMBER SIX

I am fortunate enough to love and enjoy numbers, having been a Maths teacher for many years. I was keen to discover the significance of the number six, which was particularly associated with Anusha ~ six symbols, six-pointed star, six letters in its name ~ so checked it out by delving into various books on numerology.

As you may know, numerology is the psychology and science of numbers and can be used as a helpful tool to enhance our understanding of life situations, thoughts, feelings and experiences.

Every person vibrates to certain numbers depending on their given name, date of birth etc. In fact, their soul is ascribed a particular combination of numbers, rather like a barcode.

THE PERFECT NUMBER

Each number between one and nine (any number greater than nine can be added together to form a single number between one and nine) has many qualities, both positive and negative.

The number six is connected with harmony, beauty, commitment and relationships. It is also linked with a desire to love and be loved unconditionally. Six incorporates the concept that home is of paramount importance, bringing great joy and emotional security. Significantly, it is very nurturing, and is considered to be the mother/father number. Additionally, six can denote perfectionism, since it's the first 'perfect' number, in that the sum of its divisors, other than itself, is equal to itself: $1 + 2 + 3 = 6$ and the product of its divisors, other than itself, also equals itself: $3 \times 2 \times 1 = 6$.

Using all six Anusha symbols

- *Self-healing with Anusha symbols*

Stand with feet hip-width apart and, placing both hands on your solar plexus, begin to take slow, deep breaths. On the out breath, slowly and with meaning and intent, murmur the words, "calm", "still", "peace", repeating each three times.

Visualise the six-pointed star in silver/violet light above your crown chakra and imagine streams of shimmering light comprising millions of tiny sparkling stars pouring from the star and cascading over your aura, enveloping you with healing energy.

When you are ready, draw the Anusha Master symbol, Nomada, with your tongue on the roof of your mouth and, using your hands as guides, blow its energy upwards and outwards to join the streams of healing energy flowing into your aura. You may choose to visualise the symbol instead.

Focus on your chakras and sense which chakra or chakras need this particular vibration of energy, allowing it to flow through your body bringing harmony, calm and peace to this area.

Now, at your own pace, repeat with each Anusha symbol in turn directing or allowing their unique energies to find the place where they are most needed: Hogarth ... Tabor ... Kanue ... Anja ... Anshar ...

In your own time, place both hands on your solar plexus taking slow, deep breaths. On the out breath, slowly and with meaning and intent, murmur the words, "calm", "still", "peace", three times each. Return, thanking the Divine Source and whatever spiritual beings accompanied you during this healing experience.

AT-ONE-MENT

The process of attuning others to the energy of Anusha was given to me in a dream, during which I was actually performing the process with a natural ease that made me feel that I'd always known it and had been doing it for many years. It involved a great deal of blowing, using the breath to propel the symbols into the aura and certain chakras. It also incorporated symbols being guided into the feet, perhaps as an acknowledgement of the Essene practice of anointing the feet as a symbol of respect, as well as bathing dusty feet before entering a dwelling! This also felt like an essential grounding procedure, given the floaty, starry nature of the energy.

I thought, like other energy systems such as Reiki, that it was to be called an attunement, but every time I tried to type the word attunement into my PC, it was changed to 'atonement'. I felt puzzled since I understood that the word atonement means 'reparation of wrong or injury', so hastily checked in The Concise Oxford Dictionary and discovered it also means 'a reconciliation of God and Man'. The penny then dropped that the process of opening ourselves up to receive this energy from the stars brought us into alignment with 'all that is', brought a powerful sense of connectedness, of being 'at one'. What appeared to be accidental was, of course, totally intentional ~ a clear message of the underlying purpose and meaning of the energy. Connecting with Anusha was an at-one-ment!

A note about at-one-ments ...

As with all energy systems the process of receiving an at-one-ment i.e. having the symbols placed in the aura/chakras by a Master Teacher is recommended. This activates the energy of the symbols enabling you to use them to their full extent. However, the Anusha symbols can be used to a certain degree without an at-one-ment. We invite you to try them out and, if you feel drawn to the energy, to come along to a workshop.

RETREAT TO WALES

We now had all six symbols; the complete set (or so we thought!) together with the at-one-ment process and decided to go on a retreat to a remote place in order to perform at-one-ments on each other. We felt that both our energies already resonated with the Anusha vibration yet wanted to experience an at-one-ment, particularly in preparation for performing them on others.

Trusting our instincts we simply put a pin in a map and struck gold. It landed near Tregaron in West Wales. We searched the internet for just the right place and happened upon self-catering holiday cottages on a smallholding perched on the edge of the Cambrian Mountains and close to the Cardigan Bay Heritage coastline. Perfect! Even more perfect was that it was extremely close to Lampeter, which delighted us since The Cygnus Review (a free monthly magazine reviewing alternative health and lifestyle, personal growth, spirituality and ecological books) had recently opened a shop at 2, Market Place there. We planned to visit and spend a few happy hours scouring the shelves for goodies. I took along a copy of the Review with the details of the location and a handy little map.

It was quite a journey, concluding with a meandering 40 minutes discovering then revisiting the exact same delights of rural Wales! We were relieved to arrive and settle in. We sat on a wooden bench outside the converted Victorian Coach House enjoying the earthy smells and gazing at distant mist covered mountains. The owners had a host of friendly dogs keen to welcome us, tails wagging and noses sniffing out new aromas. It was blissfully remote and quiet; it was indeed perfect!

Having settled in we walked and walked, cleared our heads and hearts of any mugginess and gradually began to prepare our energy for the at-one-ments. For some reason I felt strongly that we needed to visit the Cygnus Review shop in Lampeter before we performed the at-one-ments so searched for the magazine to find the little map. The Review kept falling out of my hand and landing with the Chat Page uppermost and, after it had done this three times, I finally got the message and looked at it more carefully. My eyes were drawn to a letter titled 'Shiva Lingams' and I felt a frisson of excitement run through my entire body. When we attuned others to Reiki we always put an amethyst of the person's choice, one their energy resonated with, under their chair or a small one in their lap, if they preferred. We definitely believed there was an Anusha crystal but, as yet, had not been given any information about it. Now we had!

Thea Holly wrote the letter and she has kindly given her permission to reproduce it here:

Shiva Lingams

I first saw a Shiva Lingam on an internet site and found it so fascinating that I bought it. After finding its energy unlike anything else I had worked with, I bought enough for a workshop I was running on Crystal Energy. Everyone felt something different with each crystal we worked with until I handed out the Shiva Lingams – then they all experienced the same unique energies.

The energies that emanate from these stones link us to the Earth and the Universe depending on which hand you hold them in. The sensations are very powerful. The energies also change when we place them either vertically or horizontally in the palms of our hands. We can also channel healing from them to another person; the energy is then experienced in waves that some people can actually see. These are very powerful stones.

About three months ago I began working with beings who call themselves the Guardians of the Golden Re. They are as old as time itself and support our personal growth and that of this planet. They told me that Shiva Lingams represent the closest physical thing on Earth to their energy. They seem to express the dual nature of these beings. Shiva Lingams originate from only one site, the Narmada River in India, and worldwide people are now waking up to their extraordinary healing energy. They are truly remarkable.

So, we had to go into Lampeter to find a Shiva Lingam! Amazingly we did exactly that and found several really easily! We held them in our hands, this way, then that, and marvelled at their splendour and powerful energy. We could both totally understand Thea being bowled over by them. We were now ready to go ahead with the at-one-ment on each other, resting the remarkable stones under the chair and in our laps.

We proceeded with a mixture of excitement and slight apprehension, casting tentative glances at the notes I'd made when the information had been given to me. My turn came and I felt a surge of light energy flash through my body, familiar yet immensely moving. I experienced the deepest sense of peace and bliss, of being complete and connected, total balance, like nothing I'd ever experienced. Images flickered through my mind's eye ... deserts, scrolls, hazy mirages, wandering nomads, gazing at stars in the night sky, star charts. I felt comfortable, relaxed, surrounded by the energy of friends I trusted and loved, at peace.

Afterwards I felt incredibly tired for many hours and Kate slept non-stop for over a day. We packed our bags at the end of our stay, knowing that something enormous had happened to us, from which we would never look back!

On our return two important events occurred. The first was that we fully realised the role of Shiva Lingams in the healing and at-one-ment process. I keenly researched them and discovered that these amazing stones were only found in the Narmada river high in the mountains of Mandhata in Western India, one of seven sacred, holy places in India, and were accessible during the dry season when they were collected from the riverbed and shaped using mud and oils. The similarity between the name of the river and our Master symbol did not escape me ~ perhaps the name I'd been given had more than one meaning or interpretation!

Geologists claimed that the stones were created when a meteorite invaded the riverbed millions of years ago. They were formed from Crypto Crystalline Quartz (a mix of chalcedony, iron oxide and goethite) and were said to contain the highest vibration of all stones on earth. Their phallic shape and distinctive markings were believed to represent the power of Shiva, the Lord of

Creation and the marks on his forehead, which are symbolic of feminine, fertile energy. Consequently, they are thought to represent the balance between male and female energy. Furthermore, I read that their energy both balanced and purified mind, body and spirit; that they specifically relate to the heart centre and are a manifestation of the love energy that we all share.

Interestingly, the stones were said to be instrumental in DNA activation and rejuvenation, to empower, to protect psychically, to enhance the attunement process and to generally improve health and well-being. They could also be used during meditation to focus energy on positive outcomes and to promote balance and harmony within. No wonder we were drawn to use them in our at-one-ments!

My reading and experience of the stones confirmed what Holly had written in her letter, that the energies emanating from the stones link us very powerfully to Mother Earth and the Universe, and that the energy changes when they are placed either vertically or horizontally in the palms of our hands. Powerful stones indeed!

I was intrigued by the mention of chalcedony, which had popped up several times for me over the previous week or so. A dear friend, Zan, who intuitively felt I needed its energy close to me at this exact time, had given me a beautiful tumbled piece. Later, whilst reading my much loved copy of 'The Crystal Bible' by Judy Hall I learned that, "Chalcedony is a nurturing stone that promotes brother/sisterhood and good will and enhances group stability. It absorbs and dissipates negative energy bringing the mind, body, emotions and spirit into harmony, instilling feelings of benevolence and generosity. It removes hostility and transforms melancholy into joy, eases self-doubt and facilitates constructive inward reflection". This very much resonated with the exquisite energy of Anusha.

The second event that occurred on our return revolved around the fact that Kate was experiencing a constant and deep ache in between her shoulder blades, which was restricting her movement. She visited her kinesiologist, Rowena, who remarked that the delicate balance of her heart chakra was disrupted. She re-balanced Kate's heart chakra and gave us the useful advice that, when giving at-one-ments, to request that all the cells of the body receive the Anusha energy easily and smoothly. This made total sense to us and we duly incorporated it into every subsequent at-one-ment.

We urge you to procure a Shiva Lingam or two ~ the right ones will call out to you ~ and spend some exciting and enjoyable time working with their unique energy.

SAY A LITTLE PRAYER

GIVING THANKS FOR ANUSHA

During our stay in the Coach House I channelled a beautiful prayer, which offers thanks to the Universe/Divine Source for this majestic energy and for the unconditional and profound love surrounding and enfolding us all as our souls evolve.

Anusha Prayer

*Thank you for the bright shining light of your love
Illuminating the depths of my heart and soul
Bringing me steadily home to myself.*

*Thank you for the calm following turbulent storms
Awakening the stillness residing within
Bringing me truly home to myself.*

Thank you for the peace in my very essence

Revealing profound faith and inner wisdom
Bringing me finally home to myself.

I am calm
I am still
I am peace

I am home

Feeling the prayer within

Set aside three days when you know you can rise just
before dawn and ensure you have everything you need
to be comfortable, so you can sit or lie for a short while.
(If this feels too difficult, then perform this ritual at any
time of the day or night that suits your lifestyle.
Whatever you choose, affirm that this choice is perfect
for you!).

To begin, find a comfortable position and take a few
moments to slow down your breathing, feeling your
belly rise and fall as you take in and exhale several slow,
deep breaths. Place your hands on your heart or solar
plexus, whichever is most comfortable and feels right
for you.

On the first day, with pure intention and feeling, repeat
three times:

Thank you for the bright shining light of your love
Illuminating the depths of my heart and soul
Bringing me steadily home to myself.

Allow yourself to really feel Divine love in your heart, in your soul and the reassuring, blissful feeling of steadily coming home to yourself. Allow yourself to become aware of any sensations, thoughts or feelings that emerge for you, without judgement, and express gratitude for them. If you wish, you may write these down or simply make a mental note of them.

Then at your own pace, as many times as feels right for you, repeat the mantra:

I am calm
I am still
I am peace

I am home

On the second day, start by repeating:

Thank you for the calm following turbulent storms
Awakening the stillness residing within
Bringing me truly home to myself.

Allow yourself to feel the restful, welcome calm after churning through difficulties, problems, hassles and frustrations and the stillness that comes after the turbulence subsides. Again, allow yourself to become aware of any sensations, thoughts or feelings that emerge for you, without judgement, and express gratitude for them. If you wish, you may write these down or simply make a mental note of them. Repeat the mantra, as you wish.

On the third day, repeat:

> *Thank you for the peace in my very essence*
> *Revealing profound faith and inner wisdom*
> *Bringing me finally home to myself.*

Let yourself become immersed in this exquisite peace, allow it to pour into your inner being and feel it releasing your infinite wisdom and faith ~ in yourself and your truth. Once again, allow yourself to become aware of any sensations, thoughts or feelings that emerge for you, without judgement, and give thanks for them. Again, if you wish, write these down or simply make a mental note of them. Repeat the mantra, as you wish.

PRESENTING ANUSHA

CROWDS GATHER AT ROSSETTI HALL!

We were now in a place to share Anusha with as many people as we could gather together in our local hall. As with all these events the relative ease of delivery, including the wonderfully decorated and brightly festooned hall, belied the hours of hard work we and our dearest friends had devoted to it. Frankie wrote a wonderfully evocative guided visualisation. Claire hand painted magnificent six-pointed stars in silver and violet on two delicately coloured lilac sheets. Both Lesley and Frankie joined us in reading the Anusha prayer. The room buzzed with the energy of fifty amazing people!

Although we'd spoken to many people about Anusha before, this marked the beginning of 'going public'! The response was overwhelmingly positive and lots of people signed up to be participate in at-one-ments.

We were delighted and jubilant; the Anusha community was forming ~ we were coming home!

PHASE 2

BUILDING THE COMMUNITY

THE AT-ONE-MENTS BEGIN

After the presentation, we truly felt part of something big, something great and growing. We felt the passionate interest of those people who had attended and had recognised the souls of many fellow Essenes as we scoured the sea of faces eagerly receiving the information about Anusha at the presentation. Interestingly, some people just knew they needed to experience the at-one-ment immediately, so we ran our first workshop within a few weeks. Others were slow burners, for example, there was a person who came along who joined us for Level 1 in June 2010, almost five years later. We totally accept that everyone has their own path to follow and they'll find their way to Anusha when the time's right for them.

One of the many huge advantages of building the Anusha community, step by step, person by person was meeting those with whom we felt an extraordinary connection ~ a feeling of meeting again after many, many years. For me, Liz Murdoch was one of those precious people. We had shared a close, inspirational and productive relationship as key members of an

Essene community, which I was to discover in a past life regression held sometime later. Liz tells her story of being at the presentation:

> *"I was fortunate enough to be invited to attend an afternoon's gathering where Kate and Patsi introduced the Anusha healing system to their healer and therapist friends and acquaintances.*
>
> *I had no idea what to expect, but found myself being totally absorbed by the story of how the symbols were brought to Kate and Patsi, and how the Universe hinted to them that Anusha is very much connected to the Essenes. I have always been interested in the mysterious Essenes and I was fascinated to learn that they had some sort of connection with this new and interesting healing system.*
>
> *At that time I was very dubious about any type of healing that apparently needed symbols to make it work, and as such I was somewhat sceptical about Reiki. What I hadn't realised at the time was that just about everyone at the Anusha meeting apart from myself was a Reiki healer. After the meeting we were all invited to book ourselves in for a Level 1 Anusha course, and when I went away to contemplate whether to take the course or not my personal prejudice against 'symbols' caused me great angst.*

I had worked for some years as a crystal healer and to the best of my knowledge I had never consciously used a symbol during that time, so for quite a few days I found myself in a great state of turmoil because my heart really wanted to follow the interesting and new Anusha path, yet my head kept saying to me, "But it uses 'symbols'! Why would anyone want to use symbols?" Every cell in my body was telling me to trust my instincts and to embrace Anusha, but my head continually tried to talk me out of it. In the end I decided to call in my guide and meditate on the problem. He'd know what to do!

As with all good guides mine is very patient with me and he listened with good humour as I told him all about my Anusha problem. I tried to be as honest as I could and explained how I was highly suspicious of any type of healing that expected me to use symbols. I was telling him how I just couldn't see myself doing anything like that when I felt his amusement grow.

"What about this?" he asked, and showed me an image of the golden ohm symbols I had painted beside the front and back doors of my home.

"And what about this?" I saw the cross that was hanging over my bedroom door.

"And this?" The dolphin necklace I liked to wear so much because of all the things the dolphin image meant to me at that time.

And so the list went on. By the time my guide had finished with me I felt like such an idiot that I couldn't help but roar with laughter at my own ignorance and sheer stupidity. I immediately picked up the phone and made the call to book myself in on an Anusha Level 1 course. And I have never looked back since!"

Liz goes on to describe her experiences of the workshop and how she worked with Anusha in the early days:

"Once I'd embraced the fact that I do indeed use symbols in my everyday life and thus overcame my prejudice against using 'symbols' I made my way to the Winter's Way Therapy Centre to participate in an Anusha Level 1 course.

Never having experienced anything quite like it before I wasn't sure what to expect from an Anusha at-one-ment. Unbeknown to me the other participants were all Reiki attuned, so the process must have been rather 'old hat' for them. I found that I enjoyed the at-one-ment process, and the coursework was really very interesting. I had lots to take away with me at the end of the course, including my first Anusha symbols, and the freedom to use them in whatever way worked best for me.

Not having been Reiki trained I knew nothing of Master Symbols, Power Symbols, or anything else, so I simply used the Anusha symbols when I felt guided to. I would use the Master Symbol either first or last, or sometimes both, depending on how I was guided. When I was guided to use it first it felt like a key unlocking a way in, when it was used last it felt as if it were placing a seal on the healing. With some clients both seemed to be required.

I have always worked as an intuitive healer and when working with crystals, my speciality, I know which crystals to place and where to place them because I can already 'see' them in position on the client's body. After bringing home the Anusha symbols I discovered that the same thing applied to them and they would 'appear' on the client's body in the place where they were most needed. So this is where I would place them, and then I would either tap or blow them in depending on what felt right for each individual client. Generally this is the method that I still use today.

Although I had only four symbols to work with I found that I could do a lot with them. I was very pleased with the grounding symbol as at that time I was finding it very difficult to keep myself *grounded. I discovered that two of the symbols combined (Tabor and Kanue) are brilliant to use with decording work, and when removing attachments of any sort. But the one symbol I seemed to be missing was one for protection. Try as I might I just couldn't see how any of the symbols would offer protection, and at that time even Kate and Pats were trying to figure that one out. Eventually it was Anushee Lesley who unlocked the mystery by revealing that she used Kanue for protection. It is a symbol that works on boundaries. When you draw it, it has seven loops, and Lesley would make sure to draw one of the loops over each one of the seven chakras, thus sealing and protecting them. I was sooo impressed! Why the heck didn't I think of that?"*

The Anusha community began to grow and we held a small number of workshops and at-one-ments over the next few months. Slow but sure. Sometimes we still needed to pinch ourselves, not quite believing the enormity of it all. Eventually, we settled into a rhythm, but it was to be short lived. In early 2006 an extraordinary thing happened ~ Kate received another symbol!

Bring on the Bull

Tora

This was not just any old symbol! It was strong as a bull, fiery and determined! Over to Kate to explain what happened:

> *"I was working with someone who felt stuck to me, and in this particular case I didn't think, "I wish I had a symbol for ...". This was slightly different, because, rather than seeing a clear symbol, I saw a bull and I heard the word Tora, which I wrongly thought meant bull, which it doesn't actually!"*

Taurus is actually Latin for bull, so the word is very similar. Also, when Kate researched its meaning she discovered that Tora is the Japanese word for tiger and also means 'attack achieving surprise' or 'stealth' and this tied in with what she'd felt during the healing session.

Kate again:

> *"I think Tora does kind of get in there and attack. Anyway, I saw a bull and I could see the bull breaking through the old patterns, almost forcing the person to let go of the old stuff. I knew, in my head, that I would be able to draw this bull in six movements, which felt really important. I could just see how these six movements would draw a bull, and it does. I knew that it was a very earthy thing, that it was just clearing away earth-based rubbish that gets in our way – ego stuff maybe."*

Maybe we had got stuck, had made assumptions about what we had, what we'd been given and needed a good shake, needed encouragement to be open and receive the possibility of more, of infinite possibilities. Maybe our egos had told us that 6 symbols were all we deserved and the reality is that we deserve everything the Universe has to offer. We were on a roll and were ready for more. And they certainly came!

Additionally, Tora is the name of a constellation of stars featuring 7 main bright stars and, significantly, The Torah is the Law of God as revealed to Moses and recorded in the first five books of the Hebrew Scriptures.

TORA

- *Breaking down/letting go*
- *Dismantling old patterns*
- *Clearing away past life troubles*
- *Addictions NB. Earth based*

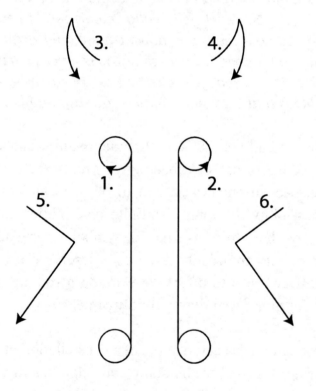

Using Tora

NB. Tora can be drawn with the fingers of one hand or you can use both, each hand drawing one side of the symbol simultaneously. This feels very flowing and engages both aspects of yourself i.e. male and female, producing a strong sense of balance and harmony.

- *To remove blocks, old outmoded patterns etc.*

When you feel stuck, have reached a block and feel you can go no further (often accompanied by a feeling of frustration and annoyance!), draw or visualise Tora over your solar plexus, then 'see' an unstoppable bull casting aside any unwanted blocks in its path. Actually visualise the blocks or a representation of them being strewn aside and an opening created for you to move through easily and smoothly. Thank the obstacles or blocks for being there, acknowledging that they were doing a job in helping you to learn something essential to your soul's progression.

When working with others, proceed similarly by drawing Tora over their torso and suggesting, if they're willing, that you visualise the bull together. They may wish to describe to you what the block looks or feels like to them so the process can become more graphic.

Send Tora to a seemingly intractable situation, particularly where old values and beliefs are blocking the way forward. This includes past life situations. Visualise as above and don't forget to acknowledge the value to your ongoing evolution of having held those beliefs.

- *To let go of anything that no longer serves you*

Proceed as above, this time visualising the thing/person or situation you would like to let go or get rid off being cast aside in no uncertain terms by the bull.

- *To eliminate/diminish the effects of addictions*

Use with Ganesha (see later).

- *To ease the pain of loss (bereavement, employment, divorce/separation, self-belief/esteem etc.)*

Use with Hogarth, Anshar, Nembula, Ganesha as intuitively guided (see later for both Nembula and Ganesha).

TALL, DARK & HANDSOME

ZARATHEA

Then, to our surprise, another symbol came through! I received this one when I was at a pamper day organised by my dear friend, Amanda, in support of the Cycle Mongolia Challenge, which she was participating in to fundraise for the National Deaf Children's Society. There was a plethora of complementary healers in the room and I enjoyed sampling several treatments, including receiving Anusha healing from one of our community of healers, Zan. She is an extremely powerful channel for the healing and I remember feeling a surge of healing energy from her hands to my gums, which had been troubling me and were painful and inflamed. They were completely fine afterwards, much to my relief!

During the session I saw the symbol very, very clearly. I scribbled it down afterwards as Zan described this tall, dark, handsome presence at her right shoulder during the session. I didn't know for sure why 'he' was there but within the next five minutes I was called over by an amazing woman, offering hands and feet reflexology, who said, "I've just got to tell you, you need to protect yourself from the mix of energies in the room. I saw you in a bubble with this amazing light all around you – something was definitely going on. You are very sensitive and need to protect and ground yourself". I guess 'he' was there to protect my energy generally from the mish-mash of energies in the room and to ground me, having received several different energy healing treatments.

This wasn't the first time that Zarathea had come. I had sensed his energy before and heard the unusual name when I was giving healing to a treasured friend, John. I sensed the presence of an exceptionally tall (taller every time I tell the story!), broad shouldered, dark haired male standing behind my right shoulder. I felt very protected, easy and safe with his energy, as if he was there to reassure or support in some way. I could smell sandalwood and thought how much I liked John's aftershave. When I mentioned this to him afterwards he declared that he wasn't wearing any! Now I know when Zarathea is with me because of his distinctive smell. Although I got a sense of his energy, he didn't give me the symbol just then. I just felt him and thought he was there for John for some reason and subsequently told John about him, without really understanding what had happened. Now, I realise that Zarathea is my Anusha guide and call upon him often, finding him utterly trustworthy, an extremely protective and comforting presence. He also wears great aftershave!

Researching the word afterwards I discovered that, to find its meaning, Zarathea has to be split into its two component parts. In Hebrew Zara means Prince, Princess and Light. Thea is Latin for gift of God/Goddess and Greek for Goddess. So, Zarathea could mean the gift of light from God/Goddess or a Prince/Princess sent as a gift from God/Goddess. So, Zarathea is our gift from the Divine! (Editor's note: Another synchronicity is that the gift of the Shivas was received from Thea!)

Zan has been spiritually and energetically aware since she can remember. She is an intuitive and experienced Reiki and Anusha Master and Gardener, particularly enjoying Lunar Vegetable Gardening. You can e-mail Zan at monadsunset@yahoo.com

ZARATHEA

- *Protection*
- *Grounding*
- *Boundaries*

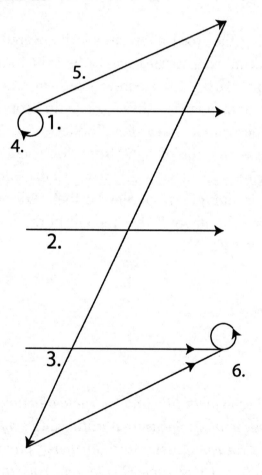

<u>Using Zarathea</u>

- *To protect your home/workplace/car etc. and establish clear boundaries around it*

Draw Zarathea in doorways, especially the front and back door of your house etc. Tap in its name three times and express, with gratitude, your specific intention, for example, "Thank you Zarathea for protecting my home and for ensuring that only the highest energies enter here".

NB. You can send Zarathea to buildings when a person living or working there feels they are currently being, or may be, threatened or attacked.

- *To protect yourself/others and establish healthy boundaries*

Place the symbol over your whole body, either in your aura or directly over a particular chakra or over the entire body of the other person. Communicate the exact purpose its energy will be serving, making it specific to that person or situation.

CONNECTING TO ALL THAT IS

NEMBULA

We realised that we were on another roll and waited with bated breath! Then Kate received her absolute favourite symbol, which fills her with tingles every time she uses it. The symbol, Nembula, came through when Kate was working with a woman who only ever came for healing on one occasion, so, clearly, part of the client's life purpose was to help bring through this incredible symbol. We are eternally grateful to her for this apparently chance encounter!

Kate summarised the client's situation by saying that she was disconnected from everything, from herself, her family, her friends and, frustratingly, from any kind of financial abundance. As the symbol emerged in Kate's mind she knew it was about connection to the infinite source of abundance. We believe that when people are in an impoverished state ~ whether it's impoverished through lack of love or material possessions, it's because they're not connected to the Universe.

So, Kate knew that, when she visualised this odd looking symbol, the unfurling lasso in the centre was about connecting to the Universe and should spiral upwards and outwards, be flung up high with verve and aplomb. The lasso would then connect to 'all that is', thus opening a clear, open channel so that abundance could flow easily and freely. As with all energy healing, intention is paramount and the act of using a symbol for any purpose automatically draws that energy towards us. Kate never knew what happened for the client other than what she shared at the end of the session ~ a feeling of calm, peace and tranquillity ~ but she began to utilise the symbol herself to impressive effect. She says with huge enthusiasm that she loves this symbol!

Since receiving Nembula our financial situation has improved massively and numerous members of our Anusha community have reported the same substantial increase in abundance of all kinds. It's interesting that many spiritual people believe that they should be poor or impoverished, needing to express their spirituality by being without worldly possessions. This is a view that may have slipped into this lifetime from previous lives as monks, nuns, hermits, holy people etc. who lived in spartan environments with very few material possessions, and we allow it to remain and continue to influence our thinking and perceptions. I'd like to challenge this outdated belief … it simply isn't true! I now believe we can have and truly deserve to have whatever we want and need to live the lives of our choice.

Interestingly, one of our community, Suse, says that she always used to forget about Nembula when running through the symbols but doesn't do that anymore, indicating that any reluctance she felt about having abundance has been removed and she's now embracing it in her life. She says she has a massive grin on her face every time she uses the symbol now. I had a similar experience. For many months afterwards, although Kate had shown me the symbol, I disregarded it entirely as if it didn't exist. Financial abundance had been my issue, having been brought up to believe I would never have money and that money was somehow wrong … filthy rich! I had constantly reinforced this belief by making sweeping statements about money; standing in the supermarket checkout and being asked if it was alright to give me a handful of change, I would respond, "That's fine, I won't have it for long, anyway!". No wonder money flowed away from me with alacrity! A turning point occurred for me whilst hearing others talk about the fact that money is simply energy, that money is love, and I began to use the symbol regularly. Now, there's no looking back. When I check my bank balance I'm always pleasantly surprised and appreciative.

Lesley, who always has an original spin on all things Anusha, called her new house Nembula. In her own words, "When I found the house I felt was mine, I drew Nembula all over the details sheet of the house given to me by the estate agents. I drew it over the whole front of the house in the picture. Every night I held the details between my hands and focused purely on sending Anusha energy via Nembula to the house and the buying process. When I had completed the mortgage application form I sandwiched it overnight between a Nembula drawn on paper and a Shiva Lingam on the top. I knew that Nembula would bring abundance and connection. I knew that I already felt connected to that house and the ability to purchase it for myself would bring the abundance. I was successful and the house became mine for exactly the amount I offered!

As soon as I moved in I called the house Nembula and I've also drawn the symbol on a small piece of paper and placed it just above the letterbox, so all my mail has Nembula written on it as well as touching the symbol as it's delivered. I have now been living in my house for over a year and have received incredible abundance. From a financial point of view, I've received significant refunds and I am in credit on all of my utility bills. I've also been blessed with an abundance of lovely new friends and feel very loved and cared for. (Trivia – I got my keys the day Obama got the keys to the White House!).

So what does it mean? Well, Kate heard Nembula, so that's what we call it, but the word's origin is probably Nebula, which is taken from the Latin word meaning 'mist' and describes the first stage of a star's cycle. In fact, it's an interstellar cloud of dust, hydrogen gas and plasma clumped together to form stars and planets. Stars again!

NEMBULA

- *Abundance*
- *Expansiveness*
- *Connection*

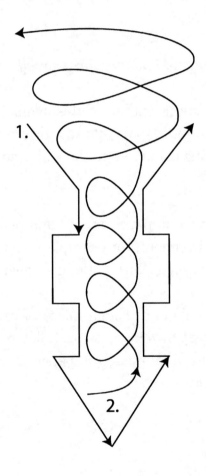

Using Nembula

NB. Again, Nembula can be drawn with both hands, thus bringing in an abundance of balancing male and female energy. You can include as many swirls as feels right for you, really throw yourself enthusiastically into drawing the lasso and enjoy the burst of feel good energy it brings!

- *Generating abundance for yourself or others*

Pour the exciting energy of this symbol into your (or their) heart centre, solar plexus, or crown chakra and visualise being connected to the Universe, to the infinite source.

Draw Nembula on paper or card and place strategically in your environment, for example under pillows, beds, chairs, on your letterbox, under a moneybox etc.

Draw the symbol on a small piece of card, credit card sized, and keep in your purse or wallet, or in your bag or pocket. You can laminate the paper or card to make it longer lasting.

New Beginnings

GANESHA

By now we had returned to a place of expecting symbols to appear and wondered aloud to each other whether we might receive twelve, two lots of six. Then along came Ganesha! Kate received this gentle yet powerful symbol when she was working with a long-term client, whose issues included feeling stuck and unable to let go. Kate reported that the symbol just appeared. By this time she knew exactly what was happening and was even getting used to them coming through. She intuitively knew this one was a companion to Tora.

In her own words, "I heard the name Ganesha, and saw what resembled the head of an elephant, and sensed this symbol was a partner to Tora. They are both animals with very distinctive energy, the raging, determined bull and the strong but gentle elephant and

I knew that Ganesha also had to be drawn in six movements in a similar way to Tora. To me they're two faces of a coin, Ganesha the spiritual side of the coin and Tora the earth, so it's almost two halves of one symbol. Anyway, I knew that Ganesha was present to clear away any spiritual issues or blocks rather than just the earth-based stuff".

Unusually, we were both aware of Ganesh and had been drawn to his energies for many years, without knowing a great deal of the story that surrounded him. So, I delved into my research, something I was enjoying more and more. I frequently found the results astonishing, the meanings of the apparently random words were always so relevant, which made the experience quite compelling.

I discovered that Ganesh is the elephant-headed Hindu God of prosperity, wisdom and remover of obstacles, sometimes referred to as the Lord of Beginnings. He was the child of Shiva, the Lord of the Dance and Parvati, Goddess of marriage and households. There are many versions of Ganesh's story; one legend suggests that Shiva and Parvati argued bitterly about having children and when their baby was born Shiva chopped off his head in a fit of rage and then, in remorse, replaced it with the first head he could find, a baby elephant's.

Ganesh has a sweet, polite, gentle yet immensely strong energy and, in a loving and protective way, uproots and discards any blockages in our path. He helps us realise that all barriers are self-imposed and reflect a fear of moving forward. Since these blocks are self-created they can also be willed away, therefore Ganesh encourages us to believe that all obstacles are surmountable.

GANESHA

- *Breakthrough*
- *Connection*
- *New Beginnings*
- *Addictions NB. Spiritual*

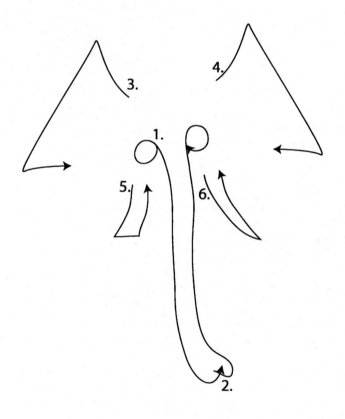

Using Ganesha

Ganesha is perfect when a problem, issue or situation feels insurmountable, obstinate and unresponsive, even (and perhaps especially) when linked to a past life experience.

NB. Use with Tora; they are companion symbols and make a formidable partnership! Tora is earth based and works with issues to do with the three dimensional world. It works with the physical issues associated with this incarnation, with ego or personality, with the illusion! Ganesha addresses the spiritual; it works with the higher self, the spirit that is one with 'all that is'.

- *To breakthrough, eliminate/minimise addictions*

When helping to break through the stagnation and crippling pain of addictions (in the broadest sense, not just addictions to drugs, alcohol or other self-harming behaviours but also addictions to certain emotions, like feeling sad, lost, angry, bitter, resentful, vengeful, stuck and so on):

Ganesha can be drawn over yourself or another person with one or both hands or focused into a particular chakra. Remember it's more the flavour of the energy rather than an exact duplicate of the symbol that you need to convey. Allow yourself to connect with elephant energy, powerful yet with a profound intelligence and gentleness, and imagine this unique energy flowing wherever it's needed.

Visualise the trunk curling around and containing the pain, distress or difficulty of the situation. Gradually, feel the negative emotions fading away and the trunk flinging any residual sediment way into the distance until it totally disappears.

- *To connect with your higher self when embarking on a new beginning*

This symbol works positively with any kind of new beginnings, so it's extremely helpful to use it when working with a proposal or ideas for a new project. Simply put a copy of the symbol underneath or on top of relevant papers and leave it to use its intelligence to do what's best spiritually.

If you're buying or selling a house, embarking on a new business or starting a relationship, personal or professional, send Ganesha to that situation. Imagine its energy overcoming any difficulties and connecting you to your inner wisdom and knowing, as well as to the source of infinite prosperity.

Guided Visualisation to meet Ganesh

Find a comfortable position, feet on the ground and begin by slowing down your breathing ... breathe in slowly and deeply and exhale slowly and easily ... do this three times ... and relax ... relax ... relax ... now take your attention to your feet and visualise roots growing down into Mother Earth and circling her inner core ... feel the pulse of her heartbeat as she sends her loving, nurturing energy back, back to your feet ... feel her love, support, strength and grounding energy fill your body, your being ... relax ... relax ... relax.

Now, visualise a six-pointed star sparkling and twinkling in pure white light above your crown and see thousands of tiny stars cascading downwards from the star filling your aura with shimmering love and light ... now, return your attention to the large star beaming above your crown and again visualise tiny stars pouring down and entering your crown chakra, then meandering downwards through your chakras ... balancing, cleansing and harmonising each chakra in turn ... crown, third eye, throat ... balancing, harmonising and cleansing ... heart, solar plexus, sacral, base ... cleansing, balancing, harmonising ... and repeat the mantra to yourself three times: Calm, still, peace ...

Now, on your next breath, transport yourself to a clearing on the periphery of a beautiful, exotic jungle ... hear the sounds of animals in loving and meaningful communication, feel the perfect warmth of the jungle wrapping around you like a comfort blanket ... and breathe, breathe it in, fill your being with this delicious warmth and you feel totally safe and secure ... at one with the sights and sounds of nature, at one with Mother Earth.

Slowly, you become aware of a presence moving towards you and, glimpsing through the verdant foliage, you see the reassuring, majestic figure of Ganesh approaching ... his long, effortless strides propelling him forwards with ease through the dense undergrowth as if it were no more than a mist.

As he draws closer and still closer, you are able to look deeply into his eyes and feel his gentle, loving gaze as a comforting, supportive embrace ... You sigh deeply as you fall into a reverie ... feeling warm, calm, safe and loved ... loved unconditionally, loved profoundly ... You feel his strength, his determination, his resolve nestling within your being, your core ... and breathe, breathe it in, fill your being with this delicious sensation of peace and strength, gentleness and resolve, calm and determination ...

In this moment of clarity, you realise that your awareness is subtly shifting, that you perceive things differently ... as you focus your own gentle gaze, your inner vision, on your life and its apparent difficulties, you become aware of a fundamental truth ... you understand that all obstacles are part of the dark illusion ... the illusion that your fear has created ... you understand that all your struggles, all your blocks are self-created, merely a manifestation of your worries and fears.

You now realise that you have the power, the necessary resources to remove these blocks and you are ready to do that right now ... visualise your fears being transformed to love, your worries transmuting to joy, your anxieties morphing into the certain knowledge that all is well. As love pours through and from you, all those problems that seemed insurmountable now fade into insignificance ... all those blocks evaporate and disappear ... and see and feel that happening now.

You look ahead and see that your path is completely clear ... you have made the perfect space, beaming with love and light, sparkling with infinite possibilities ... with Ganesh's trusty support you are now attracting new beginnings ... new energies ... new ventures ... new adventures! Ganesh urges you to say: Yes! I can do it! Yes! I can have it! Yes! I can be it! Yes, I can!

Visualise your life now, exactly as you wish it to be ... use all your senses ... see, hear, taste, feel, smell ... surround yourself with every vibrant detail of your chosen reality ... it feels easy, effortless ... affirm to yourself, "This is my life, right here, right now". And stay for a while, feeling in all parts of your being the bliss and fulfilment, happiness and pleasure, serenity and joy around you ...

Now, when you're ready, turn to Ganesh and thank him from your heart, knowing that he is always there by your side to support, encourage and empower you ...

And, in your own time ... become conscious of your breathing ... breath steadily and normally and bring yourself back into your body, take your attention down to your feet and feel your connection with Mother Earth ... move your body however you need to, to return. Stretch, wriggle your toes ... open your eyes and return to the room ... Welcome back!

LET THERE BE LIGHT

QUASAR

So, the eleventh, perhaps the penultimate symbol, made an appearance! We now know that Quasar is unusual in that it was the only one of Kate's symbols that didn't come through in a healing session. Kate has a beautiful and very special little granddaughter called Kacie, who was about two years old at the time. She had been suffering with one cold after another, and felt quite miserable. Kate remembered thinking, "I wish I could do something to boost her immune system, I wish there was some symbol I could use" and, boom, there it was! Kate told me that she was sitting on the bed with Kacie giving her a cuddle and the symbol just appeared. The symbol is glorious in its simplicity, as children are. When Kate drew it for me, all in one movement, we agreed that it looked a bit like a sperm! Her first thought was that it was about boosting the immune system and, then when we worked with its energy, we realised that, actually, it's for releasing fear. This made sense to us because fear prevents our immune systems from working.

I also had a strong feeling that it would help with infertility, which could be about fear. I had an opportunity to use it with a client, who had been trying to have a child for a long, long time. Recently I heard she's having twins! I remember her lying on the couch saying, "I'm really scared to bring a child into this world." Although she wanted a child desperately, she was holding enormous fear, which ultimately she needed to let go of. We worked together for some time, using Quasar alongside other symbols. The healing came to an end when she moved out of the area and it was a little while later that I heard the wonderful news about her pregnancy.

Now, Kacie and Layla, my gorgeous granddaughter, both have the symbol under their beds, and although they still get colds they are whisked away in no time! Kate's elder daughter, Stephanie also sleeps with symbols under the bed, including Quasar. She had flu after Christmas 2009, in a short spell between two lots of snow, and was completely knocked out by it. This was particularly difficult for her as she has a four-year-old daughter. She'd never had flu before and kept saying, "I'm dying – I think I'm dying!" and Kate said, "No, you've just got flu". Kate poured healing into her and after just four days of being bed bound, unable to move, she was out tobogganing on the fifth day! A very quick recovery, as those of you who've had proper flu will know.

Also, we used Quasar a great deal when supporting a little girl, Laney, Kacie's best friend, who was having chemo to treat cancer. She managed not to catch any of the horrible bugs or viruses going around, even though her immune system was compromised by the chemo. She has since passed and we send our love and healing support to her on the other side.

So, what does Quasar mean? Kate thought it bizarre that a symbol should take its name from the children's activity, which is the equivalent to paint balling, where youngsters run around frantically laser beaming each other! So she wasn't surprised to discover in the New Oxford Dictionary of English that a Quasar is a massive and extremely remote celestial object, emitting exceptionally large amounts of energy, which typically has a star-like image in a telescope. It has been suggested that Quasars contain massive black holes and may represent a stage in the evolution of some galaxies. Wow!

QUASAR

- *Immune system strengthening*
- *Release of fear*
- *Infertility*
- *Phobias*

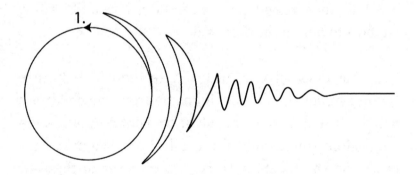

<u>Using Quasar</u>

- *To strengthen the immune system*

Draw on paper or card and place under a cot/bed/pillow.

Place the symbol over your body, over the throat chakra or crown or wherever you're guided.

- *To release fear/phobias*

Draw over the heart centre for releasing fear or phobias or find a picture that represents your fear/phobia and place the symbol on top of it.

Envisage a bubble (the sphere of Quasar) surrounding you with its tail rooted into the ground between your feet. This will eliminate fear if you feel energetically attacked or threatened and need protection from anything/one.

- *To enhance fertility*

NB. Infertility, in its widest sense, can refer to an inability to be productive or creative, so use Quasar to stimulate or restore your creativity.

Draw on the sacral chakra and/or place under the bed/couch etc.

Place under a drinking bottle, visualising its energy seeping into the liquid and enjoy letting go of your fear or blocks to fertility as you drink it.

PURIFICATION

SERPENTIA

When I received this symbol I was absolutely convinced it would be the last! It came through when I was in a temple in Thailand; I saw it really vividly and heard its name equally clearly. I instinctively felt it was very special and sensed it was about purification and spiritual enlightenment, letting go of contamination and embracing purity.

Interestingly, everywhere we looked we saw Buddhas nestling in serpents instead of the more usual lotus flowers. My daughter-in-law, Priahw, explained to me, in her broken English, that this Buddha takes care of anything to do with water and the sea, which I understand is connected energetically with emotions and, of course, is deeply cleansing.

PURIFICATION

I was on holiday, distracted by the excitement of visiting my son, Tarrick and his wife, distracted by being in a predominantly Buddhist country, and it was only afterwards, when I re-read my journal, that I realised Serpentia had been revealed to me on Easter Saturday. I was again struck by the connection with the enlightened being, Jesus, and how everything synthesised together. Easter Saturday, of course, is the day between the crucifixion and resurrection, which symbolically represents the death of an old way of being in order to make way for a radical new approach. Jesus for me represents the ultimate expression of love, acceptance and forgiveness and his way of being creates the fertile ground for peace, calm, tranquillity and bliss ~ the very essence of Anusha.

My musings about this put me in mind of an extraordinary and powerful concept, 'Radical Forgiveness', coined by Colin Tipping. In his ground breaking book, 'Radical Forgiveness: Making Room for the Miracle', Colin highlights the fact that perceiving ourselves as victims has become part of being human and that extricating ourselves from this engrained archetype requires a radical change. He asserts, "As we move into the new millennium and prepare for the imminent next great leap in our spiritual evolution it is essential that we adopt a way of living based not on fear, control, and abuse of power but on true forgiveness, unconditional love, and peace".

He goes on to say that, "Jesus gave a powerful demonstration of what transforming the victim archetype means and I believe he now waits patiently and lovingly for us to follow his lead. Up to now at least, we have failed to learn from his example precisely because the victim archetype has had such a strong hold in our psyche. We have ignored the lesson of genuine forgiveness that Jesus taught - that there are no victims. Yet we straddle the fence and attempt to forgive while staying firmly committed to being a victim. We have made Jesus the ultimate victim. This will not move us forward in our spiritual evolution. True forgiveness must include letting go completely of victim consciousness". The tools of Radical Forgiveness he offers challenge us, "to radically shift our perception of the world and our interpretations of what happens to us in our lives so we can stop being a victim".

Reading Colin's book and, most importantly, doing the Radical Forgiveness worksheets really moved our understanding forward about forgiveness and certainly enabled us to release ourselves from restrictive perceptions and the painful chains of blame and victim-hood.

So, back to Serpentia. We realised that Serpentia came through virtually three years to the day, also Easter Saturday, after we had received the Master symbol, Nomada ~ what an incredibly auspicious day, a day of deep spiritual significance! Moreover, it was given to us at a time when we were able to fully utilise it. We have used Serpentia to purify ourselves and others of negativity, to cleanse unhelpful thought patterns, to flush away blockages to forgiveness, to remove self-limiting beliefs ... a kind of soul de-tox. Ultimately, Serpentia lifts us to that longed for level of spiritual advancement, where we cease to feel vengeful and blaming, where we cease to feel judgemental, where we cease to feel different, separate and disconnected. It lifts us to a place where we feel the purity of total acceptance, the joy of true forgiveness, the delicious and delightful beauty of together-ness, one-ness.

Googling the word on my return from Thailand revealed that Serpentia is derived from the Latin word 'serpens', meaning snake, which has been interpreted as a source or deliverer of wisdom as well as encapsulating the notion of renewal, rebirth and regeneration (shedding its skin). Two snakes coiled in a double helix around a central staff form a Caduceus, which mirrors the distinctive shape of DNA, representing the creation of life as well as being a symbol of spiritual awakening. The Caduceus corresponds to the 7 major chakras, which carry our life force energy.

Given Serpentia's ability to raise vibration, to cleanse our egos, to stimulate spiritual awakening, I imagine you can understand why I assumed this was the very last symbol. We rejoiced at its power, beauty and majesty then settled into focusing on strengthening the Anusha community, on holding at-one-ments and healing as many people as possible, on spreading the word.

Colin C. Tipping is the author of the book, 'Radical Forgiveness' and the founder of The Institute for Radical Forgiveness Therapy and Coaching. His website is www.radicalforgiveness.com

SERPENTIA

- *Purify*
- *Move soul towards*
- *Enlightenment*

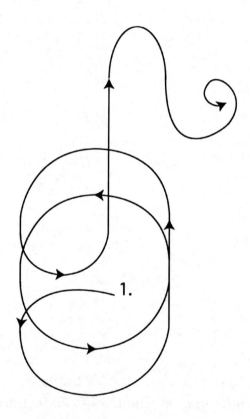

1.

Using Serpentia

- *To purify food/beverages*

Draw Serpentia on paper and laminate, if you wish, then place under food and beverages or simply draw the symbol over them. This is especially helpful when eating out, if you're in a rush and have to dash into the nearest fast food restaurant!

- *To de-tox your body*

Draw over your chakras, a small one on each chakra, starting at the base and working up, followed by a large Serpentia covering all of your chakras.

- *To raise your vibration towards enlightenment*

Use as a meditation tool, to gaze upon. Allow your consciousness to drift to a place of connection with higher consciousness, with the Divine, with one-ness. Settle there in the stillness.

Visualise Serpentia in 3D and step into it, then relax, either standing or sitting in its centre. Breathe deeply and allow yourself to feel its purifying, uplifting energy moving gradually up through your chakras. Feel the energy gently flowing through your crown and streaming upwards, connecting you with the Divine Source.

- *To facilitate total forgiveness (of self and others)*

Use Serpentia in conjunction with Anshar, Tora and Ganesha either by visualising the symbols entering your body/particular chakras or surrounding you and the person or situation that requires you to let go and forgive.

GATHER TOGETHER

We soon realised that it was important to gather together for the community to fully form, or rather to re-form. On several occasions, Frankie has regressed a large group of us to Essene times to help us all connect and access the flavour of this existence. When we shared experiences afterwards, we were amazed by the vividness of our feelings, even though sometimes the details were a little hazy.

Many described having a visceral sense of the surroundings, the heat and smells consistent with Qumran and other Essene settlements. We were wearing similar clothes and engaging in the same customs that the Essenes had, for example bathing feet, communing with angels, healing etc. A common feature was being alone within the community with a strong sense of personal responsibility, of serving, and being totally content with that. In fact virtually everyone spoke of dying peacefully with a feeling of a fulfilled life and many were emotionally moved by the bliss they'd felt and were extremely grateful that they'd had the opportunity to re-experience this quiet peace. Several people expressed a reluctance to return to their present lives!

When I had regressed to my life as Jacob I had recognised the souls of several people I'm close to in this life. One of my long-time, dearest friends Sooz was fetching and carrying water alongside me and Jules F, who was the client with whom Kate brought Kanue through, was lovingly supporting the lepers in the colony. Consequently, it didn't surprise me when several people recognised, soul-to-soul, other members of the community during the group regressions. Several of us described close, loving and supportive life connections with others, which went far to explain some of the extraordinary relationships we share in this incarnation. Perhaps of most significance was the number of us who experienced being in proximity to Jesus, listening enthralled as he spoke and feeling his infinite love and compassion. There were tears as we shared these magical experiences, experiences that drew us even closer together in mutual love and respect. We realised that the contentment we all felt as Essenes was directly related to this connectedness, the sense of community, being united as one. This insight highlighted that the all too common misery around loneliness and alone-ness is a modern condition, a feature of separation and dislocation from each other and the Source.

FOLLOW THAT STAR

Which star or stars did Anusha come from? It was at a gathering that several members of the community posed this question. Surprisingly, we hadn't really thought about it before but this acted as a springboard and I decided to meditate and welcome any incoming information. Always exciting. I was told categorically that it was the Star of Bethlehem!

I knew that the Star of Bethlehem is believed to have guided the Magi, the Three Wise Men to the stable in Bethlehem where Jesus was born, but wanted to learn more. I set about researching both the Star and the Magi and discovered some fascinating ideas. I read that the light of the Star could be seen as a metaphor for the flame of creation, which really resonated with me. Also, there was a school of thought that believed the light was actually a comet and that, based on its movement, it could have been a shooting star rather than a fixed star. It was also suggested that the Star was the great conjunction of the two large planets Jupiter and Saturn, which lasted on and off for several months. This kind of celestial event can perhaps be perceived as a sign of an impending change of massive significance. In this case, the birth of a great prophet who would irrevocably transform humanity, awakening us to our true purpose and igniting the spark of connection between us and the Divine.

And the Magi? According to legend, the three wise men were Melchior, Balthazar and Gaspar. They brought gifts of gold, frankincense and myrrh to the infant. Melchior brought a golden cup, Balthazar brought a gold box of frankincense and Gaspar a flask of myrrh, a royal embalming oil. Whilst reading this, it occurred to me, with an excited jolt, that Balthazar was one of the physical embodiments of Kuthumi, one of the Ascended Masters I was told was associated with Anusha, and yet another connection emerged.

Wherever Anusha comes from, it certainly guides us to our own awakening and allows the bright light of love within us to shine. It helps us to connect with the fundamental meaning of our existence, to recognise our spirit and not lose ourselves in the illusion of our ego-based earthly existences.

STAR GODDESSES

I researched information about Goddesses linked with the stars following a request from a member of the community and felt strongly guided to the compassionate energy of Tara and mysterious energy of Nut.

Tara originated in India and her name means, 'star'. She is an immensely compassionate Goddess who calmly and lovingly guides us through the turmoil of life, steering a clear path and helping us to find our inner stillness, peace and strength.

Nut, which is pronounced Noot, is the Egyptian Goddess of the night sky. She urges us to allow mystery into our lives; to trust ourselves sufficiently to relax and leave space for the unknown to thread its way into our experiencing, knowing that we only let in whatever we want and need for our journey to wholeness, for our highest good and greatest joy.

Connecting with Anusha Goddess Energy

I wrote the following guided meditation so Anushees could have an empowering experience of Goddess energy at an Anusha gathering. I incorporated into this meditation the reference to embracing the mystery ~ the great unknown ~ with confidence, feeling safe and centred, without fear, as a means of supporting members of our community as 2012 approaches. As the Mayan calendar comes to an end we have no clear idea of how things will change. However, we strongly believe that whatever happens can only be positive, that Earth and her inhabitants will be presented with an opportunity to embrace a welcome era of peace, co-operation and unity.

Before you perform the meditation, it may be useful to read it through and practice the hara breathing. The hara, which is about an inch in diameter, is located in the belly, just behind and below the navel, about two inches in. Hara means 'sea of energy' and is considered to be the centre of the etheric body. You can imagine it like a ball of energy or consciousness, which expands as you breathe in and sends the energy to all parts of your body/being as you exhale.

Relax and take slow, deep breaths ... in and out ... in and out ... in and out. Gently place both hands on your hara area as you continue to take slow, deep breaths. Now, on the out breath, slowly and with meaning and intent, murmur the mantra, "I am calm ... I am still ... I am peace" three times.

Visualise the six-pointed star in silver/violet light above your crown chakra and imagine streams of tiny sparkling stars pouring down cascading over your aura, enveloping you with healing energy.

When you're ready, visualise this healing light flowing into your crown then gradually caressing each chakra in turn with the exquisite feeling of absolute stillness, peace and calm ... crown ... brow ... throat ... heart ... solar plexus ... sacral ... root ...

Now, Anusha healing energy surrounds and fills you ... look around and you become aware of Tara and her compassionate, calming presence, holding and supporting you ... take a deep breath to the count of 6 inhaling into your hara, your centre. Hold the breath counting to 3 and focus on the sensation. Now, exhale again to the count of 6 from your hara, feeling the air exiting as you let go. In a moment you will be ready to begin hara breathing, breathing from the centre of your being.

As you inhale allow yourself to feel centred, focused, alive. Whilst holding the air in your hara experience the busy-ness of life moving away from your calm, focused centre. When you exhale actively let go of whatever you no longer need.

Now, we are ready to do this together 3 times.

In ... Hold ... Out ...
In ... centred, focused, alive ... Hold ... Out ... let go of whatever you no longer need.
In ... centred, focused, alive ... Hold ... Out ... let go of whatever you no longer need.

Let yourself fully experience the feeling of being centred, knowing that you are only a breath away from feeling still and strong.

In this centred place of strength and stillness, allow yourself to feel at one with the enormity of Nut's body, with the night sky, stretching out above you. As you glance upon her enigmatic beauty you notice that she is smiling at you. She beckons to you, indicating a ladder of shimmering 6-pointed stars that sparkle brightly and illuminate your way. Tentatively, you step onto and climb the stairway of stars.

You become enveloped by the darkness of the night sky, surrounded by the unknown, as you feel yourself gradually drawn towards her. Finally you are nestling in her arms, immersed in her warm, comforting embrace.

You open your heart to her and experience an intense connection, trusting and enjoying her mystery.

You feel a profound sense of oneness with the unknown. In this moment, no matter what the unknown holds for you, no matter what challenges lie ahead, you feel still and calm, peaceful and safe. You remain with Nut until you feel ready to return, ready to move on ... confident and fearless.

In your own time, slowly retrace your steps back along the glittering stairway of stars, back to Earth, back to the light. As you return, you feel Tara's love, compassion and nurturing holding you, enfolding and embracing you. You sigh with a deep sense of peace and serenity, knowing all is well.

Gently, return to waking consciousness, thanking Tara, Nut and the Divine Source for this healing experience. Open your eyes and look around the room, noticing familiar things. Welcome back.

PHASE 3

FINDING THE HOLY GRAIL

THE ELUSIVE FINAL SYMBOL

DE SANGRAEL

At this point we felt we had all the symbols and were enjoying using them in our healing sessions, often combining various symbols to powerful effect. We were holding no expectation at all of any more symbols coming through. Kate was healing a client who had struggled with quite severe dyslexia and dyspraxia when, quite suddenly, a symbol appeared without her going through the usual routine of wishing for it! The symbol was extremely clear and Kate heard its name, which she reported sounded like 'De Sangria'.

Kate knew that the symbol was, on one level, to treat what she referred to as 'neurological issues', which could include conditions along the autistic spectrum. She had heard the word, which she thought was 'De Sangria' over and over in an insistent way, much more so than any of the other symbols. Kate said it was being 'thrust' at her, so she knew she had to take notice and add the symbol to the healing system. The name confounded her and all she could think of was the Spanish drink, Sangria. Delicious, exotic but not really relevant to our healing system!

When Kate reported all this to me, I was surprised and I must admit a little peeved, having just updated all the manuals to include twelve symbols and organised the at-one-ments logically into three levels. I quickly acknowledged that this was totally unimportant compared to the stunning energy of this new symbol, the lucky thirteenth! As we worked with the symbol and shared it with others we were thrilled at its panoramic scope and soon realised that its potential was massive. As well as working with dyslexia and dyspraxia, autism (including aspergers) it seemed to balance the hormonal system and could therefore be used with issues around the menopause, puberty, PMT etc.

Also, we discovered that it had yet another gift to give, that of delving into the depths of an individual's experiences and bringing to the surface any unresolved issues that the person might have. Dealing with the heavy sediment, which tends to sink to the very bottom of awareness and gets left behind, lying dormant for a whole host of reasons including the fear it holds, so it tends never to be dealt with and released.

After performing an at-one-ment on each other to the symbol's energy we both experienced a bit of a meltdown and laughingly agreed that it should come with a government health warning! Kate's meltdown was embarrassingly public for her. We were facilitating a FILM (Finding Insight and Learning through Movies) group and were discussing issues around loss and bereavement. Kate mentioned that she had lost a child twenty odd years earlier and, much to her bewilderment and indeed horror, she suddenly broke down into floods of tears, sobbing uncontrollably.

She subsequently described the experience as happening on two distinctly different levels. Although her body was wracked with grief, her mind was actually thinking, "What the hell is going on? I've dealt with this. Why can't I get control back?". However, for the rest of us as observers, it seemed like Kate was totally out of control for several minutes. Suddenly, as quickly as it had begun, the emotional storm subsided and she became her normal self again. Afterwards, Kate felt strongly that something held deeply in hibernation had been released. Previously, she'd been in therapy for years, dealing with this very issue and believed she had processed it sufficiently, that it was no longer a 'button' that could be pressed. We concluded that the symbol had facilitated this letting go at an altogether deeper level than Kate had previously experienced.

Whilst sharing it with others, one of whom was a native French speaker, we were made aware that 'sang' means blood. Ultimately, a member of the community investigated possible meanings and discovered that the symbol's name was in fact De Sangrael, which means 'of the Holy Grail'. From that point everything fell into place. It was the elusive something missing for each person ~ the thing that every one of us searches for in our lives. We realised that the symbol enabled each individual to tackle and let go of whatever they needed to. It was the catalyst that triggered the surfacing of the thorny issue or issues that had been holding them back or keeping them stuck in a place of less than total awareness, less than fully functioning. Therefore it restored flow or movement in the person's soul growth.

Looking at the symbol, Kate identified that it had three levels ~ the centre loop representing the spirit, the surrounding semi-circular shape, the mind, and the outer square-ish container, the body. Mind, body and spirit. De Sangreal therefore contains and addresses all three aspects of a person's being and experiences, bringing them into harmonious flow and healthy balance. We prioritised performing at-one-ments to the energy of this final symbol and were given feedback that it had produced amazing results. Only those people who were ready for and willing to experience the full power of the clearing process were affected in this way. Others received the energy in reference to a specific issue, for example a hormonal imbalance, and also spoke of highly successful outcomes.

So, definitely for the last time, I researched this extraordinary word and found that in Old French san gréal means 'Holy Grail', so therefore de sangreal means 'of the Holy Grail'. According to the New Oxford Dictionary of English the Holy Grail was the cup or platter used by Christ at the Last Supper, and in which Joseph of Arimathea received Christ's blood at the cross. Legend has it that Joseph of Arimathea sent it with his followers to Great Britain and founded a line of guardians to keep it safe.

Fictional works, for example 'The Da Vinci Code' and 'Holy Blood, Holy Grail' are based on the idea that the real Grail is not a cup but the womb and later the earthly remains of Mary Magdalene (Jesus' wife), plus a set of ancient documents telling the 'true' story of Jesus, his teachings and descendants.

The quest for the Holy Grail features prominently in the legend of King Arthur. In most versions the hero must prove himself worthy to be in its presence. In later tellings, the Grail is a symbol of God's grace, available to all but only fully realised by those who prepare themselves spiritually, like the saintly Galahad.

DE SANGRAEL

- *Providing whatever we most need, the elusive 'something' missing for each individual*
- *Working with residual issues*
- *Restoring fluidity/flow*
- *Correcting imbalances, especially hormonal e.g. PMT, Menopause, Puberty*
- *Dyslexia, Dyspraxia*
- *Asperger's Syndrome*

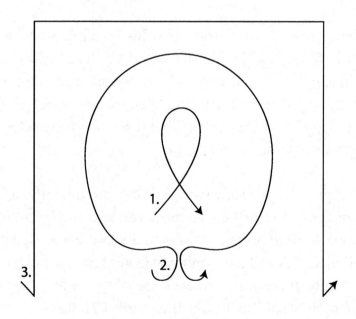

<u>Using De Sangrael</u>

There are three distinctly different ways of using De Sangrael:

Place over the crown to help with neurological issues associated with autism, aspergers, dyslexia, dyspraxia, etc.
Draw over the sacral chakra to help with hormonal imbalances.
Use as intuitively guided to tackle any residual issues, restore flow/fluidity.

LUCKY 13

THE NUMBER 13

So, we now had thirteen symbols and were very aware of the reputation of the number thirteen as bringing or causing bad luck. We decided to look into this tradition and find out for ourselves the reasons why this was the case.

For Christians, the number thirteen is thought to bring bad luck. The superstition stems from the Last Supper where Judas Iscariot was the thirteenth guest to sit at the table and would later betray Jesus, leading to his crucifixion. Norse mythology has a similar superstition; the myth suggests that twelve deities sat down at a feast for the Gods only to have Loki, the God of mischief and disorder, join them, causing one of the Gods to die during the meal. One hypothesis about the origin of Friday the 13th as an unlucky day is attributed to this being the day that the order went out for the Knights Templars to be slaughtered.

We were fascinated to read that the Egyptians actually thought that the number thirteen brought good luck! They believed that there were twelve steps on the ladder to eternal life and knowledge and to take the thirteenth step meant going through death into everlasting life. Also on a positive note, thirteen was once associated with the Epiphany by Christians, since it is believed that Jesus was visited by the Magi on his thirteenth day of life.

Interestingly, there are thirteen circles in Metatron's Cube, which is constructed by connecting the centres of the circles with straight lines. Metatron is believed to be the highest of the angels and served as the celestial scribe. In early Kabbalist scriptures, Metatron supposedly forms the cube from his soul. This cube can later be seen in Christian art, where it appears on his chest or floating behind him. Metatron's cube is regarded within Sacred Geometry as one of the most sacred patterns in existence since it contains all the information pertaining to the creation of life.

Liz M has something very interesting to say about the number thirteen:

"When the 13th Anusha symbol arrived, Frankie and I were about to take our Anusha Master Teacher course, and we had a conversation with Patsi and Kate about the significance of thirteen.

If I remember rightly we wondered if somehow, although twelve is the important basic number, later perhaps a more-important hidden 13th is revealed, perhaps only when we are ready for it, when we are able to understand its full meaning. To understand the 13th we need to have embraced and understood the twelve. We tried to think of examples of this other than the Anusha symbols.

I think someone mentioned the twelve apostles, and I mooted Judas as the possible hidden 13th. Did you know that although the church made Judas a scapegoat and held him up as an example to all of everything that is bad in this world, many religious scholars actually hold a different view of him? It is believed that Judas was in fact simply following Jesus' orders. Both Jesus and Judas were well aware of what the outcome would be, and Jesus spent time with him to convince him to stick to the plan, because Judas actually didn't want to go through with it. He knew that he was to be the instrument of Jesus' death and wasn't convinced that he was strong enough to bare the burden of the outcome. Which, as it turns out, he wasn't. Poor man. Certain scholars feel that far from Peter being Jesus' closest apostle and confident, it was actually Judas who was the closest and most trusted by Jesus. So here is an example of the 'obvious' *twelve, yet the real truth of it lies with the 'Hidden 13th'.*

I suppose you could say that this principle of the Hidden 13th could also apply to our monthly calendar where we keep track of our earth's annual rotation around the sun. We have our man-made calendar of 12 months which is shoved into our faces every day as the 'truth', but when we look deeper, or more to the point, when we look up at the moon we discover that the actual truth is that our earthly year is neatly divided up into 13 lunar months, the Hidden 13".

THE MERKABA

It was 4am and I woke up feeling a pressing, though not unfamiliar, sense of urgency and knew I needed to re-visit the energy of the Merkaba, which had been an essential aspect of the training I'd done with Angela McGerr several years before. Although I'm certain that experience had a colossal impact on me energetically, I believed there were gaps in my understanding, knowledge and experience and felt I needed to fill them. I remembered that Angela had recommended books by Drunvalo Melchizedek, 'The Flower of Life', Volumes 1 and 2. So, I got up and ordered them there and then. When they arrived and I flicked through their numerous pages, I noticed many precise and beautiful geometrical diagrams and drawings. I felt an emotional reaction to them, they made my heart sing ~ these were definitely the books for me!

I could hardly put them down; they inspired and stretched me whilst answering many questions that had hovered in the corners of my mind for some time. Volume 2 contained detailed instructions about how to activate your Merkaba together with the understandable advice that experiencing this with a qualified teacher is the best option. Melchizedek made the point that the Flower of Life facilitators are trained to help participants realise that being in a place of unconditional love is necessary, that the experience requires both knowledge and love, the balance of the left and right brain, male and female energies.

I immediately logged onto the Flower of Life website and discovered a teacher who had trained with Melchizedek called Amarna Sinclair. I was thrilled to read that she offered workshops entitled 'The Teachings of the Merkaba and Sacred Geometry' both in Glastonbury and Dorset. For several reasons I was unable to travel to join her at one of these workshops, so rather cheekily asked her if she could come to us, if I could get a group together. Much to my delight, she kindly agreed. Conveniently, she had a son who lived locally and could stay with him whilst teaching the course ~ as always, the Universe had led me to the right person! We were all set, a group of exceptional Anusha Masters; we counted the days in excited anticipation. Three more participants also joined us on the course, who we thoroughly enjoyed meeting, adding a wealth of richness to the proceedings.

So, you might be wondering what a Merkaba is.

The Merkaba is the human light body ~ Mer means light, Ka means spirit and Ba means body ~ a living light body energy field that extends about 17 metres around a person's body. Melchizedek explains that the Merkaba is alive, that it's actually not a separate entity but is synonymous with the person, existing as a connection to the Divine, a unifying source. As such, it is said to carry the consciousness directly to higher dimensions, to the unified energy field of which we are all a part. In fact everything in the Universe has a Merkaba around it, not just humans. It is created or activated using a special breathing technique and meditation, utilising the principles of Sacred Geometry. The technique needs to be practiced daily until the Merkaba becomes permanent and the person feels supported and surrounded by unconditional love.

Finally, the much-anticipated days arrived and Amarna began by uniting us in prayer and inviting in the energy of the Ascended Masters and other Spiritual Beings. Throughout the two days we chanted, prayed and sang in unison with verve and resonance, although, in my case, not always in tune! Amarna explained and demonstrated the fundamentals of Sacred Geometry before guiding us step by step through the process of pranic breathing and meditation to activate our Merkabas, then tutored us in programming them. The experience was breathtaking, far exceeding all my expectations!

We were particularly stunned when Amarna channelled Archangel Michael to pass on answers to some of our probing questions. We sat in absolute silence, hanging on his every word! Activating my Merkaba, though on paper had sounded very complex, under Amarna's experienced, clear and sensitive tuition actually felt surprisingly easy. Afterwards I practiced every day, relishing each blissful love-filled moment, until my Merkaba felt permanent. I could feel its presence and thought about it daily. Throughout this initial period we met as a group for support, sharing our queries and discoveries, sharing our achievements.

With my Merkaba in place I felt subtly different, totally in tune with my heart, much more open to loving myself and others and generally more connected to everyone and everything. It was the perfect extension to the Anusha experience, taking me to another level of ascension and perhaps an aspect of my own Holy Grail.

Amarna Sinclair is a facilitator for the Flower of Life, a Kwan Yin Magnified Healer and Trance Channel for the Hierarchy. She trained and worked with Drunvalo and it is her joy and passion to pass on his teachings - the MerKaBa meditation and Union with Higher Self, facilitating the ascension process, leading to total enlightenment. She is happy to travel wherever there is a group ready for this wondrous step. You can contact her on amarnajoy@googlemail.com or 01202 699579.

ACCOMPANIED BY THE MASTER

REBIRTHING & SANANDA

I was suddenly taken with the desire to experience healing from somebody entirely new with a different approach and way of working. As per usual I woke at 4am and scurried to the computer and began to google practitioners in the local area. I was driven! I didn't know quite what or who I was looking for but did know that I would instantly recognise the person when I found them! Eventually, I heaved a huge sigh of relief when I discovered a woman living quite locally who sounded warm, loving, versatile and talented.

I booked a two-hour slot on Friday, 11/9/09 (a significant date?) and arrived, feeling open and welcoming a fresh and exciting new experience. Nikki had picked two oracle cards for me before my arrival and both were highly significant. Oshun and Eostre from The Goddess Oracle pack. Nikki lovingly encouraged me to talk a little about myself and I felt instantly trusting of her. Having tuned into me energetically, she intuitively felt that Rebirthing was the way to go and I agreed enthusiastically.

So, Nikki settled me comfortably on sumptuous cushions and thick, soft blankets on the floor and sprayed an Australian bush essence into the air around me, placing a mysterious green crystal near to my head. Normally, I'd be inquisitive about knowing its name but had no need and just snuggled into the cosy blankets and relaxed.

We began the breath work and my first awareness was of agonising pain ... in my left ankle, below my left knee, starting at my lower rib cage on the left side and gradually moving around the front until it was level with my solar plexus, then my heart centre. I breathed into the pain until it subsided and I could feel my initial resistance waning until, quicker and quicker, I completely let go and allowed myself to go with the flow. Instantaneously I was transported to the desert ... I was Jacob the Essene ... I was dying. Sananda first stood beside me, then kneeled at my side, still seeming tall and straight with his head bowed towards me. He held my hand and a delicious warm glow, like warm treacle spread through my hand, arm and entire body. He spoke in hushed tones yet I heard him clearly. He called me 'my son' and assured me that he was constantly with me.

More than five years before when I was regressed to this same life I had the sense that The Messiah was there "to ease my passing" and knew that this was the moment. He gestured with his free hand and a golden orb appeared and surrounded me. It filled with light. The light was almost filigree, like candy floss, a pale pink-violet colour. The light flowed in swirls into my heart and I was filled with the most exquisite peace and calm. I remember thinking, "This is what bliss feels like", as I floated into the swirling light. I felt no pain and knew I was passing. I felt part of everything ... oneness. Sananda told me that I could feel like this whenever I wanted and I believed him!

Nikki added this:

> "I first met Patsi in September 2009. She wanted to shift whatever was blocking her from living her truth and asked me what I had to offer that was different from what she had experienced before. It was clear to me that she had done an awful lot of inner work and I felt intuitively that together we may be able to do something.
>
> All I really did was to facilitate a safe space for Patsi to open to the intelligence of her own Soul. I took her into that space through gentle rebirthing

breathing. Immediately she accessed a past life, one in which she knew and was close to Jesus. The interesting thing here is that I have always worked with the Christ energy and I have a powerful picture of Sananda (Jesus) which I had felt it important to keep out and show to Patsi. (At this point I didn't know about "Anusha" or the connection with the Essene community.)

On the second session, Patsi channelled Sananda. I was deeply touched by the purity of love she was undoubtably experiencing as well as the peace which filled her heart. It is my belief that Patsi and I were brought together (having known each other in at least one Essene life-time), to spread this wonderful energy further into and beyond our community. I have since been initiated into the Anusha healing system and it is already affecting my life by gently helping me to retrieve the lost parts of myself. A series of magical synchronicities have since woven their way through my life like a golden thread of hope. The interconnectedness of all beings is becoming more apparent to me thanks to Patsi, and our sessions have certainly deepened the Soul work that I do."

Nikki offers Psychic/Tarot/ Soul Contract consultations and various healing therapies, releasing blocks to Soul growth to support the Spirit on its journey. She can be contacted via her website www.souldivination.co.uk and on 07810 787899. Please see the July/August 2010 edition of Kindred Spirit for a 'Question and Answer' interview with Nikki.

PERMISSION GRANTED

PASSING OUT NOT OVER!

My next challenging yet awesome experience was on a Saturday night after a week's de-tox and a colonic irrigation. I meandered into the kitchen to make a drink, became dizzy and light headed and keeled over. I smashed my chin on the floor, ripping it open, bright red blood gushing everywhere. I was out cold for maybe two to three seconds yet I was convinced it was an age. In the darkness I saw a man approaching me along an extremely long, shadowy corridor and, leaning into me, he spoke quickly yet gently about my future. He told me that the time was now. It was Sananda!

After a trip to A & E and gluing of the gash I spent three weeks feeling dizzy and light-headed, often fearful of passing out, before I finally got up one morning feeling perfectly fine as if nothing had happened. I realised

Sananda had been talking about the writing of this book and I suddenly felt optimistic and positive about its completion. However, the time was not quite now since we were headed into a period of intensity, of powerful energy pouring through a cosmic portal created by the alignment of stars and planets between 11/11/09 and 29/11/09 ... 11.11.11. I slumped into fatigue for eighteen days, bought two new pairs of pyjamas to chill out in and relaxed. I didn't start any new projects or ideas and simply waited, recharging my batteries and allowing my mere mortal body to absorb and assimilate the extraordinary energies coming through. This was followed by a breathtakingly powerful full moon, which laid me out again for a couple of days. I woke in the night with whisperings in my ear and knew I'd have new knowledge by the morning! I guess I was ready then because I sat down and wrote ... and wrote ... and wrote!

ANUSHA

EXPERIENCES

Our community has grown and, at the time of writing, numbers 67. Each person has a fascinating and often incredible story to tell about his or her experiences of Anusha. I include here just a few with loving, appreciative thanks to the writers. Enjoy and be inspired!

ANUSHA EXPERIENCES

DARRYL'S DREAM

"Have you heard of Anusha?" a friend asked me over coffee, "no" I replied. My friend Sue started to explain some of the principles and foundations surrounding Anusha, I was instantly intrigued ... a relatively new form of healing channelled only in the last 6 years, that's a secret lost art and over 2000 years old. Comparisons were made to Reiki healing which I'm au fait with, but not in a pros and cons way but instead how it assists and heightens healing energies. It sounded awesome ... Sue and I parted, I felt on top of the world as I walked home. I don't think my feet touched the floor, I simply glided or floated. Later that night I couldn't help but think if I were to master this art could I raise the profile and take it to a bigger stage? I've co-written a TV show about healing which is in pre-production stage and hopefully coming to TV in 2011.

Was Anusha a path for me, was my show being stalled so that I could learn Anusha? I found the two Anusha Masters who channelled the art on Google that night; they live about 5 miles from me, coincidence? I sent them both an email explaining how I wanted to be a part of the next workshop being run. The excitement running through me was unbelievable, I just hoped that the buzz in my email would be captured and I wouldn't be dismissed as some sort of random emailing at 03:00!

A few days later Patsi replied, I could feel the warmth and love in her words as dates were provided, she couldn't wait to meet me and I was invited to a healing share evening in the up and coming weeks.

It was the night of the share, I'd been at work all day so hoped that I wouldn't be grumpy or more concerning, fall asleep! As I arrived, the energy emerging from one particular house told me, hmmm this must be the place. As I entered, the vibrations in the house were so high, my head almost exploded, I found Sue and clung to her, as she was the only person I knew there. The energy in the room was intense. It was a remarkable experience; I'd never been in a room with so many healers. The company was great, somewhere where I felt I belonged, I didn't have to hide behind some persona, I was me. Patsi and I spoke at length and in the group work I made sure I stayed with her and Sue. The group healing was incredibly powerful ... I could feel my guides behind me, supporting me, as I was getting so dizzy at points, without them I would have fallen off my chair. I could not believe the power that was being magnetised in the room, I day dreamed about the 15 of us loading into a mini bus and touring the world jumping out at every town, village and city and doing a quick group session and then on to the next place ... what impact would we have on the world?

Before long it was the day of my Anusha level one at-one-ment, I had remained in email contact with Patsi but had not seen her since the night of the share; I was pleased to hear my friend Sue, who was now an Anusha Master Teacher, would be assisting in the at-one-ment. I arrived at the Rossetti Hall in Holmer Green for 10:00; again the vibrations as I entered almost sent me reeling back two paces. I found a seat and before long we commenced. After a couple of guided meditations, relaxed, chakras open we were ready. I received a powerful visualisation, one of my guides, a young Native American girl, entered the room before me and kissed me on the forehead, I instantly knew I was on the right path and today was about my destiny.

I couldn't believe the sheer power of the symbols. I've completed my second degree in Reiki and studied various other forms of healing and have received some incredible success stories from healing clients, but this was something else. We were asked to practice the different symbols on one another and there are two experiences I want to share. I won't name the symbols, as I don't want to taint your experience of them, as I'm sure you'll want to experience your own feelings for yourself. As I was receiving one particular symbol from Ian, I felt like I was being pulled up from my chair, I wasn't in an altered state, I was very aware. It brought me no discomfort so I ran with it ... my hands remained on the arm rests and my feet were firmly on the ground, but I was lifting. When we finished we were invited to talk and discuss our experiences. Ian looked a little shocked as he described the feeling of having to push me down into my chair, although he could see I wasn't physically moving. He also said that once he'd finished he looked and his hands were 2 inches above my head, whereas when he'd started his hands were placed on my head.

There was another symbol that Steph used on me, this took me straight out of the room and placed me walking through a field of roses and being immersed in the most unexplainable feeling of unconditional love. I admit I'm not really an emotional person and rarely express my emotions, but seriously I could have cried at how happy and loved I felt ... even today some months on when I just recall that moment a smile breaks out over my face, the same as if I recall a funny/happy memory or something as simple as my daughter and I spending time together and particular photographs of her. It was so lovely.

Anusha has changed my life in so many ways ... I feel so at peace with myself and everything around me, it's like nothing matters any more, everything is so circumstantial in life and people dwell on the smallest things and reap havoc and misery in their own lives ... The love I experienced from that one symbol for 5 minutes confirms to me that there is more than worrying about your next phone bill ... who cares? You have no idea what is round the corner for you but I urge you ... to take the step and see for yourself. I wish you all the best in your own journey ... and may you awaken to your true path and fulfil your destiny. Love and light.

If you'd like to follow Darryl's journey or ask him anything regarding Anusha or healing contact him on: info@411ge.co.uk | twitter.com/darrylkempster | facebook.com/411GroupENT

DEBBIE'S DIARY

I was introduced to Anusha at a Shamanic course in the shape of Patsi, a lovely lady, vibrant and very personable. 6 months prior to this course, I remembered asking the Universe to find me some like-minded spiritual people, a teacher or group would be even better, and I got all of the above! It's funny how things work out.

I had already done my Reiki Master level before I worked with Anusha and I was ready to embrace a wider spiritual direction. Spiritual energy has always touched my life, whether through people, animals, nature or events, I met Patsi at a time when a chapter was closing so what better way to start a new chapter than through the sublimeness of Anusha?

What Anusha has done for me and my clients is bring a sense of self back. Working with the Anusha symbols I have found that many clients experience 'inner meditations' and some have had 'flashbacks' of past life experiences, only fleetingly but remembered. I myself have experienced a past life flash back when Patsi gave me a one-to-one Anusha healing session. Why this happens is uncertain and it isn't always experienced by everyone, but clearly, for me it was for inner personal and soul development and needed at that time.

Anusha is in some way the new Reiki, both being equal in their importance today. The Anusha symbols are many, all of which serve in healing society's modern conditions and problems. I have my favourites of course, yet they all help to heal the soul of old habits and fears. I use the symbols much as I would use Reiki; one particular client mentioned it was like being hugged by a big warm blanket! Funny that, as I used one particular Anusha symbol that signified exactly that!

Anusha is a very subtle tool for self-realisation, like Reiki, its energy is empowering and immensely humbling to receive. Reiki is the Yang while Anusha is the Ying. I use both and feel very privileged to do so. Anusha works on all levels and strangely yet amazingly it has led me to develop a deeper understanding not only of the Universe but also of people. Anusha has brought me so much and has become part of my life in many ways. I am immensely thankful for the friendships I have made and the clients I have helped. Namaste.

Debbie works as a busy holistic therapist, her skills include helping others bring balance and harmony into their lives through Anusha, Reiki, Reflexology and Massage. Debbie loves all things spiritual and spending time with nature, her family and friends. You can contact her on: mystic.beaver@hotmail.co.uk

IAN'S INSPIRATION

Ian wrote the following to me, for inclusion in this book:

"What is it like?" is a question I have been asked several times, about Anusha; and I have replied that it is like a cross between Reiki and Shamanic healing, or that it is like Reiki on steroids. I feel that a more intriguing question is posed if the last word is dropped, so that it becomes "What is it?".

My predominant memories of our first Anusha session are my initial visualisation, and the recollection, a couple of days later, of a forgotten childhood trauma. At the beginning of the session, I moved quickly and easily into that very relaxed, but hyper-alert state, that I regard as the fourth state of consciousness – in which it becomes easier to access my intuitive sub-conscious, and to connect with my true self. Immediately, I was in a desert landscape, of parched earth and bleached wood and bones. A faint trickle of water appeared over a precipice in the middle distance, as a feeling of loving, and being loved, began to envelop me. As the feeling intensified, the flow of water increased, until the landscape was transformed, by a waterfall and river, into an oasis of lush, green vegetation, accompanied by an experience of overwhelming love. I subsequently realised that it is a love that I had not experienced before, that had no specific source, nor was based on devotion to a specific subject. Initially, my ego couldn't handle that, so translated it into love passing between, and connecting, the two of us.

After returning to the normal, waking state, you mentioned that Maisie, a spirit guide, had spoken to you, saying that I needed to revisit something that happened to me when I was seven years old. Although, at the time, I could remember nothing momentous, two days later, I awoke with a clear recollection of the relevant events. Martin, my brother (usually referred to, within the family as Marty), and I were play fighting; being considerably older than me, it was a one sided affair! Trying some judo, he threw me across the room, and I hit my head hard on the tiled hearth. Martin panicked, pleaded with me not to tell our mother, and fled the house. Concussed, I sat in a chair, and closed my eyes, reopening them several hours later, with no concussion, or headache – not even a lump on my head from the impact. Perhaps unsurprisingly, during the ensuing years, I had only a vague recollection of these events, and was never entirely sure whether they were real or imagined.

In 2005, as part of a series of personal, spiritual development retreats, I completed the Enneagram psychometric test. It is the most accurate of such tests that I have completed, precisely describing my intense desires for control and independence, expressed through a strong, uncompromising and unemotional personality – which, it suggests, stems from being betrayed in childhood, by a close family member. I do not regard my episode with Martin as betrayal (which, in my opinion, entails premeditation, rather than an impulsive reaction to an accident), but the suggestion resonates profoundly with me, as explaining my development for the following forty years. It also explains the emotional desert I created for myself – because, for many years, in my view, to love (or, indeed to experience any other intense emotion) was to become dependent, and therefore vulnerable.

The healing and recuperative powers of meditation are things that I have recently begun to rediscover, through my practise and study of yoga; but the recollection of that intuitive recourse to meditation, when I was seven, and of its miraculous effects, has provided me with profound and powerful impetus.

Our first session, then, focused on my past.

My wife, Jo, joined us for our second session, at which time, I felt great, in terms of my mental, emotional, mindful and spiritual well-being, but I had a cold, that was the latest in a series of mildly debilitating physical ailments, which had continued for several weeks. Although I quickly relaxed into a highly receptive state, my relaxation was initially inhibited; it seemed by my physical condition. As my congestion cleared, and my breathing came more easily, I experienced again the feeling of universal love (albeit, my ego attributed it to you and Jo!) – but this time, with an introverted aspect to it, where I was able to receive love, but felt unable to contribute (or, from an egoical perspective, to reciprocate). At first, I struggled – trying to be an active participant (a vestige of my difficulty in graciously accepting the unreciprocated generosity of others) – but realised that, on this occasion, it was important that I received, but didn't give (not only because of my physical condition, but also for my mental, emotional, mindful and spiritual development).

During the session, you and Jo saw Snake and Bear Cub with me. The particular significance of the appearance of these Power Animals was, in the case of the former, death (of old, decrepit ideas and attitudes) and rebirth (of new, better ones), and in the case of the latter, the need to preserve my sense of fun, and to accept that new ideas and attitudes may take two years to mature (the time Bear Cub stays with its mother) and (forgive the pun) bear fruit.

Our second session, then, focused on my present.

At the beginning of our third session, I immediately became what, at that time, I considered to be fully relaxed, and became acutely aware of the feeling of overwhelming love, and of the healing energy embodied within it. As you directed the Anusha healing energy to different parts of my body, their symbolic significance became very clear to me. Foremost among these were my heart, shoulders, knees and ankles; my shoulders being where, metaphorically, I have often chosen to carry the responsibilities of (and for) others – a propensity which dissipated, as my shoulders relaxed; my knees and ankles are representative of my lack of physical flexibility – their reluctance to fully relax being indicative that the further development of, not only physical, but also mental, emotional, mindful and spiritual flexibility, remains, for me, work in progress!

A lot of healing energy was directed to my heart, which, I am certain, has enabled me to understand the true nature of the universal, loving energy, which, for me, is Anusha. You may recall that some words came to me, that I have subsequently refined, and, I believe, improved, so that they have become: "Whatever the issue, the best response is love." Also, I am beginning to appreciate and understand the tautology inherent in the phrase "unconditional love".

It is appealing, in terms of symmetry, to suggest that our third session focused on my future; but I feel that it actually helped me to focus, to a greater degree, on my true present (rather than the egoical version, to which I am habituated).

I have experienced Anusha as true, universal love, but, to return to my earlier question – "What is it" – I believe that Anusha has given me glimpses of true reality (rather than my version of it); so, intriguingly, the answer is, perhaps, derived by again dropping the last word: Anusha is what is.

The very best of tools is, of course, only as good as the artisan who wields it. I believe that a supreme exponent of any art can intuitively be recognised and appreciated by everyone. I believe that you are a supreme exponent of Anusha – and of the art of being gorgeous (although I concede that I may be biased!).

I have been contemplating why I have chosen to experience Anusha, at this stage, of this lifetime. For a while, my favourite question has been "What would I do, if I truly believed that everyone deserved the very best?" I have now amended it to "What am I feeling, when I believe that everyone deserves the very best?" I have no doubt that the transition from an emphasis on doing, to simply being, and the realisation that the answer is love, is largely due to Anusha, and your practise of it, with me. The student is ready, and the teachers have come. Om shanti.

From Monday to Friday, Ian continues to reform the construction industry, towards a more spiritual approach. At weekends, he enjoys exploring the principles of Nature Intelligence, down on the herb farm. In his spare time, he likes to expand his personal spiritual boundaries. If you wish to contact him, you may, at ian.hawkridge@dudleysmith.com

---

JUDITH'S JOURNEY

I first met Patsi in 1997 on an Indian Head Massage Course. At the time I was working as an Astrologer and practising as a Reiki healer and teacher.

Prior to this in the early '90s, not long after the harmonic convergence, I had been introduced to a group in Devon led by Joanna Prentis and Stuart Wilson, who were involved in channelling and past life regression. During my time with the group we received much information about the planetary transformation that was taking place and the collective healing that we all needed to go through in preparation for the changes to come. Most of this information - along with incredible love and compassion - was coming to us from the Ascended Masters. We were told that the Earth would be going through many changes as she was approaching a dimensional shift – some people were calling it 'Ascension' - and that by 2012 many of the great cycles would be coming to completion and a new age be born. 2012 marks the convergence of our solar system's 26,000 year orbit of the Galaxy, the Earth's precession into Aquarius, the end of the Mayan calendar and the completion of the cycle of the 4 great ages of the Aztecs, who say that the Earth will be entering into the fifth world. What amazing times we live in! One of the reasons that the Earth would be going through such changes was because our solar system was moving into an area of excess photonic activity coming from the centre of the Galaxy, called the photon belt. Through the process of its travelling through the photon belt, many things would accelerate, including our own individual and collective karma, meaning that we would be going through much karmic clearing that would involve huge physical and emotional upheaval. In order to help us deal with the negative energy that would be released during this process we were told to invoke or meditate on silver-violet light which would transmute the negative into positive energy. The Ascended Master St. Germain is known as the keeper of the silver-violet flame, and we could call upon him for support through the healing and transformative process. We also had amazing support through the love and compassion coming to us from Sananda, Mary and Kuan Yin, wisdom and guidance from Master Kuthumi, and constant love and support from the angels and a whole host of other beings who are concerned with the Earth's transition.

This group felt that they had been members of the Essenes in previous incarnation/s and much of the past-life regression was spent uncovering information about the life of the Essenes. In January 1995 a few of us went to Israel to undertake some Earth-energy work. We had been told that the Christ Light needed to be re-activated into the Earth's grid and we were guided on how we could assist in this by using crystals programmed for the purpose with love and intent. We were also given directions where this needed to be done. It was an amazing trip that culminated in me having the opportunity to swim with dolphins for the first time in my life! Being close to dolphins is an incredible experience; it feels as if their communication is transmitting pure love in the form of light energy directly into your cellular system.

Whilst in Israel, we paid a visit to Ein Gedi and to Qumran near the Dead Sea, both documented as the sites of Essene communities. Being in these places was a very emotional experience for us all. Also, visiting ancient un-named sites and walking in the desert, and sometimes sleeping out there under a clear sky filled with myriads of bright stars, was re-awakening powerful memories and connections for me on a personal level. I had always loved spending time under the stars and when I returned home I spent hours in my garden star-gazing, listening, communicating and allowing myself to really feel the energy of the stars and to hear their music. The symbol of the six-pointed star took on a particular significance for me and that was when I began to meditate with it.

When I started teaching Reiki in 1995 I wanted to bring to my classes the wonderful new information I was getting from the stars and the Ascended Masters, but it was not the time or the place. Reiki was little heard of in those days, let alone photon belts and dimensional shifts! The Masters advised me to devise a specialist course which I would call Reiki ✿ Plus aimed at those interested in learning about esoteric and higher-dimensional aspects of healing. It includes working with the merkaba (6-pointed star), light body attunements, meditations to anchor our higher chakras and energy work with crystals.

I lost touch with Patsi after the IHM Course until out of the blue last year (2009) Patsi contacted me to say that she was interested in my Reiki ✿ Plus course. She told me that she was working with an energy healing system that comes from the stars called 'Anusha'. Imagine my delight at reconnecting with Patsi after 12 years, and also to find that she was working in areas that I felt very connected with. We arranged for me to run a workshop for Patsi's Anusha group. At the same time, I was feeling very drawn to learning more about Anusha myself, and I asked Patsi if she and Kate would teach me. When I went along to an introductory talk that Patsi and Kate were giving on Anusha and we were given the opportunity to experience its energies, I knew immediately that I wanted to learn it.

Anusha healing energy is very different from that of Reiki. For me Reiki feels Earth-connected, whereas Anusha is channelling the energy of the stars. The first thing that really strikes me about Anusha is how intuitive it is. Because of that, and because of the dimensional shifts that we are going through, and the direction that is taking us in as human be-ings, I see Anusha as very much a healing system for the future.
Everything devised by the Universe is so timely! Reiki connects us to the Earth and is supportive and comforting as well as grounding. It came at a time when humanity desperately needed a tangible and coherent system of healing. It is still so relevant for bringing balance in chaotic times. Reiki is now accepted by mainstream health care organisations as a respected complementary health system and is accessible to everyone. Anusha, too, has come at the right time, to help us to move towards the realisation that we are multi-dimensional beings and our potential is limitless. While Reiki flows within a structure, Anusha is pure

intuition. Reiki is very relaxing, while Anusha seems to take one to a place of deep stillness. Reiki empowers; Anusha brings a sense of wholeness, of being in that place of what is and knowing that it is ok. As healing practices they both complement one another. I feel that it is helpful to have already done or experienced Reiki before doing the Anusha training; it is like doing the ground work first, making good your connection with the Earth before reaching out for the stars!

Anusha, like Reiki, incorporates the use of symbols. When we were shown the Anusha Master symbol on the introductory evening I instantly liked it. We were each individually given another Anusha symbol which was placed in our energy field. The one I received was de sangrael. This symbol is said to provide what we most need, the elusive 'something missing' for each individual. It restores fluidity/flow. Over the following days I felt enfolded in feminine energy. It was quite emotional and releasing, in a gentle not unpleasant way; all I wanted was to be surrounded by and express soft, feminine, gentle qualities. It was a moving and beautiful experience.

Initially, after my first at-one-ment, I felt quite wobbly as if some deep part of my brain was adapting to these new symbols; it was like I was literally trying to 'get my head round' them! Perhaps that was why Patsi had intuitively brought in De Sangrael for me on that first evening: to help prepare me to let go and be totally receptive.

I find some symbols have an instant effect such as to relieve pain or to bring a positive affirmation immediately to mind. They each have their own unique resonance and are not like Reiki symbols at all; they don't even feel like them. You can tell that they come from a different source completely.

Receiving my first Anusha treatment was amazing! Within 24 hours it had taken me to such a different space. When I went for the treatment I was feeling very tired and weighed down by everything. Immediately at the start of the treatment Sananda came to me with a message channelled through Patsi. Though I had been in a deeply relaxed state through the rest of the treatment, I remembered every word afterwards, which made it very 'real'. During the treatment tingling was going on all through my body – as if the sparkling energy of the stars was entering and rippling through my cellular system! Throughout the rest of the day, my mood was transformed. Some tearful emotions came out briefly and I was given completely the right space in which to release them. But it was more that over 24 hours my energy had gradually changed from over-burdened and stressed to joyous relief, and I felt immense support coming from the universe. It was a really positive experience.

On a personal level, I find Anusha like a breath of fresh air. It comes at a perfect time for me. I have reached a certain point of equilibrium within myself, but at the same time I am aware that there is still so much more to learn and to do. I feel that Anusha has come to reconnect me with some part of myself that I have yet to re-member and fully integrate which will help me walk forward into the next phase of my life.

I spent many years in my earlier life exploring the esoteric pathways of Eastern, Vedic and Yogic traditions, acquainting myself with gods and goddesses from Indian and Tibetan spiritual traditions - including Ganesha, Shiva and Tara - and experiencing the power of meditation and mantra. The wheel has turned full circle and here I am again, re-visiting these old friends and bringing them all together under the umbrella of Anusha – Gods and Goddesses, angels and Ascended Masters, the stars and planets, and my own healing/spiritual journey. It feels so timely and appropriate. I feel a huge heart connection with Patsi, and through Anusha I feel that the Essene connection too may fully reveal itself and perhaps re-awaken memories held deep within. It is really exciting! I have always wanted to write and Anusha is inspiring me to get on and do it. I feel energised and alive and full of ideas! Yet at the same time, Anusha does give me this wonderful sense of peace, stillness and calm.
I really do feel that I am coming home.

Judith Clough is a Diamond Path Reiki Master Teacher, Anusha Master Teach and an Astrologer. She also runs courses in Crystal healing and Shamanism. Judith is passionate about helping people to feel empowered and inspired! She offers healing treatments and courses for self-empowerment and spiritual development in the UK and abroad. Judith lives near Amersham in Buckinghamshire and can be contacted at www.judithclough.co.uk

---

LESLEY'S LIAISON WITH ANUSHA

From the moment of the at-one-ment I felt a different connection to that of Reiki. I remember feeling utter peace and total calm almost like time had stopped and everyone and everything was paused.

The body has a point where it exists calmly and peacefully between breaths. With relaxed breathing you can find a point between the in and out breath where life and energy continues to flow with no issues and no panic and no stress. Anusha to me feels like this point in time. Total peace, total calm and inner knowing that all is well.

During the at-one-ment I was aware of a sensation of warmth around my feet. My guide came to me very clearly with Anusha and this guide is a wonderful silver grey wolf. The relationship I have with this guide encourages me to feel with my heart and listen to my intuition.

Being predominantly auditory, to have a guide that doesn't speak in words is a continuation of my learning, even though mildly frustrating at times. Whenever I engage with Anusha I still feel the warmth at my feet.

Anusha "star" energy is truly cosmic. Allowing it to unfold within me and around me, whilst being willing to accept things grander than I have ever imagined, helps change my direction as I step into the next phase of my original "soul blue print". Anusha guides the way to being my true, authentic self, linking me with my true, authentic purpose and, whilst gently surrendering the smaller and more diluted version of who I thought I was, places me there more readily. I am absolutely FINALLY coming home to myself.

Lesley is a Master Teacher of both Anusha and Reiki. She has been on her spiritual journey for around 10 years now and "delights in passing on energy, tools and therapies that I know work because they work for me everyday." www.reikiatnembula.co.uk

LIZ E'S LETTER

When I first trained to become an Anusha healer, during the at-one-ment, I felt a deep warm heat within my heart that spread through my body, and felt a profound sense of stillness and peace like I had never felt before.

Each symbol felt very powerful and using the symbols has had a remarkable effect. Hogarth was one that I used quite often as I suffer from migraines and it definitely calmed my pounding head and kept the headache at bay.

The Nomada symbol feels so homely and peaceful and I have often used this on myself when I have felt anxious and noticed an immediate difference. It has slowed my thoughts instantly. I also use the symbol in the house when cleansing and I always feel my home is very calm and peaceful.

I combine Anusha with other therapies that I use, including Indian Head Massage, and always have very good results, my clients report feeling a tremendous sense of peace and tranquillity. And I feel this too. It also goes very well with Reiki and seems to blend well with the Reiki symbols.

I have trained to Anusha Master Teacher level now and this has been a tremendous leap for me. My life has changed dramatically since doing the training, so much has happened. I was writing a lot of poetry from March to Sept '09, influenced by completing my Anusha Master course in May.

I know Anusha has given me confidence, much more then ever before. I facilitated my first workshop around that time and knew that this was only the beginning for me and that this was what I loved to do. I also published a book of poetry and inspirational writing at the end of '09 and, when looking at what I have written, it is very much based on the principles of Anusha. Having found an inner peace I no longer feel I need to search outside myself to be truly happy and content. Everything in my life has fallen into place for me now – I have finally found my way home within myself, and I thank Anusha for this.

Liz also kindly agreed to share the following powerful Anusha healing experience:

When having a healing session with Patsi, we discussed issues around my feelings of rejection. Patsi suggested that I used the Anusha symbols Ganesha and Tora to really release and let go of old patterns and Serpentia to purify and move my soul towards enlightenment.

Patsi said to do this healing every day for 3 weeks, so I decided to represent the 3 weeks by using 21 crystals and build a special altar at home.

On the first day using the symbols was incredibly powerful and another word kept coming into my mind, it was De Sangrael, the 13th Anusha symbol, which gets deep down and clears old residue. I consulted Patsi and we agreed that I also use this symbol in my healing.

The feelings of rejection had stemmed from me being adopted, and over the years other incidents occurred that magnified these feelings and triggered these emotions that physically brought out migraines that occurred frequently throughout my life, from the age of about 10 years old. Now at 42 years old, I felt it was finally time to heal and confront this issue, to finally put it to rest.

In each healing session I meditated and imagined all the people that I felt had rejected me throughout my life. In turn I forgave each person and myself and accepted that the situation needed to happen. I trusted my intuition and let the words and affirmations flow that I used in this healing. I replaced the old hurts with love and peace each time.

After 14 days I started to feel lifted and more peaceful and happy again, for a while I felt I had been slipping back into depression.

On the 14th session, instead of needing to forgive, I could see ahead a set of marble steps and an angel standing at the top waiting for me. I knew that this next week would be to reach the top and that I would be free.

Also, I'd had a lot of trouble with my boiler system over the last 10 years, and at this time I was having a brand new boiler fitted. The amazing thing was that it was to be finished on the last day of my cleansing period – the 21st day. I knew this was relevant, as I knew that everything going on around us is a reflection of what is going on inside of ourselves. A brand new boiler, and a brand new me!

So for the next 7 days I concentrated on taking each step further and further towards the angel, I felt calm and more in control. On the 21st day as I reached the angel she handed me a scroll which I carefully rolled out and it had written on it, "You are loved, You are liked, You are special, You are chosen". She then handed me a beacon of light to show me that I will shine eternally.

I sat and with my hands in the prayer position and thanked all the angels, my spirit guides and all the healers in the Universe. I truly felt special at last!

Liz Everett is an Anusha Healer/Teacher, Inspirational Writer – Author of 'An Inner Light That Shines So Bright'. Liz helps others to shine their light in her creative workshops. You can contact Liz Everett at www.ladybirdlodge.me.uk

---

LIZ M'S LOVE FOR ANUSHA

Although I am now a Reiki Master/Teacher as well as an Anusha Master/Teacher, my passion is always for Anusha. There are no strict sets of codes or dogmas to be adhered to, no specific order in which symbols must be used, and nothing to be kept hidden. Unlike Reiki you are not required to keep the names of the Anusha symbols under wraps, you are quite free to sing their names out loud and allow their light to shine on all. Anusha has a symbol for everything, and everyone and anyone may embrace them, with or without the benefit of an at-one-ment. Anusha is a healing system for this age, and we Anushees have been waiting a long time for its re-emergence.

I am calm (nearly)
I am still (nearly)

I am peace (very nearly)
I am home (absolutely)

Liz Murdoch is a Crystal/Reiki/Anusha Healer and Master Teacher. She resides in what she considers to be the most amazing spiritual sanctuary, the Isle of Man. She may be contacted at: lizmurdoch62@manx.net

---

NATALIE'S NEWS

My children, Lewis and Jena are 5 and 2 and are fascinated by Anusha healing. They love the comfort it brings when they hurt themselves, or awaken in the night either upset or in pain, as it soothes them back to sleep. They enjoy feeling the warmth from mummy's hands.

Before they go to sleep I bring out my Anusha manuals and they choose a few symbols each, which I draw on paper and place under their mattresses. They choose different ones each night, however both of them always include Quasar. The children don't know what they mean, but instinctively seem to know which ones will help them. Quasar strengthens the immune system, so you can understand with all the coughs and colds that go around, why they are always drawn to this symbol.

Lewis has really come along leaps and bounds. He had a poor immune system due to asthma and food intolerance when he was younger, and always had a few weeks off nursery or school here and there when he couldn't shake off illnesses going round. Since I have learnt Anusha he is hardly ever ill, which is fantastic and such an improvement from the pale, ill little man he used to be. He has also come out of his shell at school, and his confidence has improved tenfold.

Jena has benefited from having more sleep, and I hardly noticed her teething stage as it went so smoothly with the assistance of Anusha. If you could bottle Anusha and sell it in the supermarkets with all the other teething products, it would be a sell out!

Natalie is a holistic therapist offering Anusha, Reiki, Indian Head Massage and Facial Massage. She is passionate about learning and developing herself and is currently working towards becoming an aerobics instructor. You can contact Natalie via www.therapies4women.co.uk

PAT'S PASSION

Looking back I can't remember exactly when I started my Anusha journey. I only know that it was something I had to do. My at-one-ments were pretty spectacular! I was taken to the most beautiful peaceful place. The grass was green; the sky was blue; the sun was yellow and the flowers covered every colour of the spectrum and beyond. But these colours were not like colours I had ever seen before. Vivid doesn't even come close. There was a train passing in the background. I have a much better understanding of that train now. All the passengers are people whose paths I've crossed this time round. This was the start of my incredible journey.

By the time I completed my Anusha Master Teacher, lots of things had changed in my life. The ongoing struggle to clear the things that no longer served me suddenly took on new dimensions. Anusha enabled me to look at issues from different angles and perspectives.

Whilst having a choice of symbols to work with, I found myself drawn to some old favourites! I was spending time with people with very negative energy - not by choice! The reality is that they will always be in my life and I needed to find a way of keeping things manageable. Tora to the rescue! I visualised this powerful symbol 'charging' round my solar plexus severing ties, and moving everyone back a few paces. We all have people in our lives who drain us. I find Tora invaluable!

I moved house with very little furniture and no television. I stayed with friends for a week before the move to my new home and slept with Nembula under my pillow. Imagine my surprise on moving day to discover at the last minute that my sellers decided to leave sofas, lounge furniture, dressing tables, chests of drawers, rugs, dining room table and chairs, kettle, toaster, Dyson, smoothie maker, juicers, cupboards full of crockery, his and her bikes, 2 cross trainers, more beds than I had rooms to put them in, curtains and blinds - not to mention 5 televisions! Go Nembula go!

Anusha has travelled to the south of Spain. The area has attracted numerous alternative therapies and I have been fortunate to host some healing gatherings in my home. On one occasion, a friend arrived very distressed as her brother in law was in hospital in the UK. His condition had deteriorated during the day and he was too ill to have invasive treatment. He had received the last rights and the family were with him. All except his brother who was unable to get a flight for a couple of days and feared he would arrive too late. We put a photo on my jasmine healing tree - with Nomada - and sent distance healing. The next day a message arrived to say that he'd rallied – this enabled him to spend quality time with his brother, sort out lots of unfinished business and to die peacefully, in his sleep, some 10 days later.

This year, with a fellow Anushee, we were blessed with the opportunity to give healing to one of my neighbours who has a myriad of physical problems. She described a feeling of peace and stillness covering her like a blanket. Some days later, we hosted a healing share, and once again people were using the words soft, peace, stillness, calm - and a very specific claim that it was 'different'!

A friend returning to the UK suddenly took ill with stomach cramps just an hour before leaving the house. I gave her some healing - using Kanue and concentrating on grounding and protection. Within 10 minutes she said she felt fine.

I personally use Zarathea more than any other symbol. It has always felt so right for me - from the moment Kate let me have it early!!! It felt a bit like raiding the biscuit tin - and being frightened of getting caught – I've just used it as much as I could! Interestingly - before I left the UK – I completely Zarathea'd the entire house - every nook and cranny and all doors - including outside. My neighbour was burgled within my first week away .... coincidence? This gentle giant protects me and my houses and makes me feel so incredibly safe.

Anusha has quite simply empowered and enlightened me. I feel more connected to some people - and surprisingly have ended up getting rid of some very negative and draining people in my life - people who have been around for decades! In some ways it has enabled massive clear outs of both things and people who no longer serve me.

Having Anusha in my life feels like being wrapped up in a healing blanket. I never had this feeling with Reiki. I feel ... I know that I am a better person for having 'belief' in my life. I don't care where the source comes from - but I know that I can make a difference – sometimes ... and that's the only thing that matters.

I now feel supported, protected and very safe - and even on darkest days - never ever feel alone. My amazing guides walk with me every day. This is something that just seems to gather momentum. I don't know when this started - it's without labels and time tags - which sort of sits right somehow. My intuition is honed - I am more aware of cosmic shifts - I have a million miles still to travel ... and the rest ... Anusha is the most powerful tool in my resource box. How blessed am I?

Pat is an Anusha Master Teacher and Reiki 2 Healer. She works as a freelance Drama Therapist, Teacher and Healer in the UK, Spain and Poland. She facilitates monthly healing shares at her UK base in Tyne and Wear and healing gatherings June - August near Malaga in Spain. Contact Pat at Patbrudenell@hotmail.com

---

RITA'S WRITING

I have found the whole Anusha experience quite mind blowing, very spiritually enriching and liberating, like a divine breeze that blows through the heart and mind, opening the third eye and connecting the soul to a beautiful source.

I felt this especially with Nembula -and feel it now, just by looking at the symbol. The notes I made say: Nembula, a feeling of lightness and expansiveness, connection to the Source, an out of body experience, at home with the stars.

De Sangreal is another symbol that I find especially significant. I was so very excited and a little overwhelmed when Patsi and Kate were describing the symbol at the at-one-ment and then, when we did welcome in the Holy Grail, it came with a gentle rush and a power that felt inevitable. It is a truly lovely symbol that you could get "lost" in and live in.

At at-one-ments I feel very blessed to enter a special landscape, seemingly of the Essenes, certainly a place where the Anusha Masters and Angels meet in communion. It is a desert land but not at all bleak, with opportunity to speak with the Masters and meditate on high rocks bathed in starlight and moonlight.

During the Level 3 at-one-ment I "saw" myself and a group of Anushees at Avebury. We did have thrones, but it was quite informal. Clearly ceremonies had taken place but, at that moment of seeing, we were milling around, chatting and being sociable with one another. I have the strong feeling that Anusha was used in ceremonies of Ancient times.

Stars now have a special significance; I long enjoyed them through White Eagle teachings. Now when I wake at night I draw the curtains and ask for the healing power of the stars to bless me, my family and friends - the world!

Practically, I have experimented by calling in Anusha energy, not calling on the Nomada symbol, not drawing symbols on the hands and only drawing symbols in the air around the person being healed and it is not so effective.

However, I have found the Anusha energy flows freely and with great heat when the Nomada symbol is drawn on the roof of the mouth with the tongue, and then the symbols chosen to work with are drawn on the palms of the hands.

Rita is a healer, herbalist and homeopath who makes flower essences and fragrant balms full of natural ingredients. Her website is www.beautifulbalms.com

SALLY'S STORY

My Anusha journey began in August 2008, over two years ago, although it seems in some ways much longer. I can barely even remember what life before Anusha was like now. I first met Patsi at a shamanic workshop earlier that year and we both had a very strong connection with each other from the moment we met. When Patsi suggested I come along to the Anusha level

1 workshop and explained a bit about what Anusha was, I felt resistance. I had no desire to take part at all and so was a little surprised when I found myself contacting her to say I would come. When I was asked at the workshop why I wanted to learn Anusha I had no answer to give, which is not like me at all. I always painstakingly weigh up everything I do and have to have more reasons to proceed that not.

Then I received my first at-one-ment and have never relaxed so deeply whilst still conscious, in fact probably not even when asleep. I thought I might fall off the chair I was sitting on, but somehow stayed on it, although I sank down and kept finding my shoulders moving further and further down and backwards. While we were eating some fruit afterwards Patsi asked me how I felt and what I had experienced during the at-one-ment. I could hardly speak and could find no words to express how I was feeling, but I knew that it was lovely, if not a little disturbing, because it felt so unfamiliar. I didn't know what to think. In fact I didn't want to think at all. Where had that little voice in my head gone? It was quiet for the first time in my life. I finally came back to reality enough to drive myself home.

In the few weeks following this amazing day I was on cloud nine. Nothing bothered me and I felt I had come home every time I used the Master symbol. I know Patsi had told me that experiencing Anusha was like coming home, but the reality of feeling it first hand was so reassuring, safe and peaceful. An experience that no-one can actually tell you to be, or make you feel, just by using the words. When I went back to the follow up meeting, however, I came back to earth with a bump. Now the challenge had started. My perspective on life then, was that everything was a struggle and in that way I wasn't disappointed. Somehow, though, this time I had the strength and determination to push through this facade and create a new perspective for myself. While talking about the last few weeks and how positive I felt, my asthma kicked in and got worse and worse. I used my inhaler, but it didn't work. Kate tried healing me and it relieved the discomfort a little, but it came back not long after she stopped. I was so disappointed and confused.

Why didn't it work? It took me a long time to work out that whatever help anyone gave, I had to allow myself to be healed. In fact the best way is to realise that you don't need to be healed and connect to the feeling that you are whole already. Anusha helps you to do this. I did feel a strong sense rise up in me that this was all okay and I would gradually defeat this enemy. The mere fact that I saw asthma as an enemy to beat is very telling. When I left their house, my breathing started to ease, the further I got away from it.

What I was starting to realise then, what I now know for sure, is that I was challenging my core beliefs and part of me was resisting with almost as much determination. I didn't want to resist any more, but didn't know how to change my bodies and mind's programmed reaction. I didn't want to be this way and I was going to change. So I went to Patsi for three healing sessions. The first two didn't make a lot of difference, just enough to keep me moving forward. The last one had a deep and long lasting effect on me. It did happen slowly and has been a real roller coaster of a ride, but the highs have allowed me to keep the momentum going. This energy wasn't going to gently dissipate in the way I would have liked. It was going to explode out of me and keep coming back until I gave up the resistance which attracted it.

During the last treatment Patsi suggested that I ask myself why I felt trapped in the place I was now. So I did and experienced a series of visions, dreams, past-life remembrances, whatever you want to call them. Each one showed me a different way I could or had been trapped. They were so realistic that I nearly shouted out in the middle of one particularly disturbing experience. For a long time after this I pondered on what I had seen and felt. It touched me somewhere very, very deep within me.

In November 2008, we were driving back from my daughter's birthday dinner celebration when my Dad, who has been very unwell for a long time, suddenly got too cold and was shaking quite violently and uncontrollably. My first thought was to use Reiki, as that was what I was most familiar with. This had no effect on him whatsoever. It then occurred to me to try an Anusha symbol that is used for shock and trauma (Hogarth). As soon as I sent this energy into his system he stopped shaking and although weak felt a lot better. I was astonished at the sudden change, there was no doubt that the Anusha symbol had had an instant and amazing effect on him.

Shiva Lingams, I discovered, are very useful when you want to have a conversation with someone, which you worry, will not go well. They seem to help you find the right words to communicate what you mean to say. They calm down a conversation if it becomes heated, with neither party listening to the other. To achieve the best effect both people hold one, but even if you just hold one yourself it helps you to express yourself much better.

I also found two other symbols (Tora and Anshar) had a profound effect on my asthma, able to stop an attack in its tracks and keep it away for quite a while. However, after a period of time, their effect became less and less. I was a little confused, but eventually realised that whilst these symbols help to release the energy blockages causing each condition, you must still change the pattern of belief and behaviour that create the blockage in the first place. It was time for me to delve deeper and discover what in my own personal case asthma meant to me. Even when I worked this out, I still had to keep reminding myself and let go. It sounds so easy, but we often have something invested in staying the way we are. It provides an excuse for us to get out of doing something that we want to do but are scared of. So I had to address that too.

I have other health issues I wanted to deal with as well and often scattered my focus so I lost momentum. Each time I just regrouped and carried on. The following February in 2009 I received an at-one-ment to Anusha level 2. This time I was more than ready for the experience and loved every moment of it and more to the point, I felt in control of what I was feeling. This doesn't mean I was in control of what happened to me, you have to actually let go of trying to control your experiences to feel happy. I mean that my feelings no longer overtook me, swamping my very being, so that I used to feel I could barely operate in every day life. Now I can feel emotions without being ruled by them. I found that as soon as I had completed level 2, I wanted to move on to level 3. I felt ready and luckily for me so did someone else, as Patsi needed at least two people to take part. So only a few weeks after the level 2 workshop, I was now doing level 3, less than a year from not wanting to do level 1! Isn't life great, you never know what is going to happen next. If you want to change your life for the better, then just state what you desire to yourself and sit back and see what turns up and go with it. You may just be pleasantly surprised with what comes along.

Again I found level 3 easy to assimilate and took the whole experience in my stride and decided to complete the teaching workshop as well. Another incredible experience. Performing an at-one-ment on someone is a totally different experience from receiving one, it felt so powerful and the confidence it gave me was immeasurable.

Meanwhile, in every day life my roller coaster was still whizzing along. I wanted to change my basic programming and that was proving to be difficult. However, I had asked for this and I began to realise that the situations that were cropping up were not random, but were appearing to me for a reason and were in fact the perfect way for me to grow and expand my understanding of myself and how I respond to certain people and situations. It took a great deal of courage, but I started to stand up for myself. I didn't want these same patterns to keep on repeating in my life, so I had to change my approach to them. I had to act in a different way. And so I did, tentatively at first and a few events knocked me sideways. They had to though, to get my attention. If I didn't pay attention to the whispers, then they got louder and louder until I could no longer ignore them.

I had finally had enough and had at long last come to the obvious realisation that I deserved better and that I was the only person who could make this happen. My first steps in a new direction were awkward to begin with. But as I started to get some positive results, my steps got bigger and bolder. Now, I (mostly!) embrace each unpleasant situation, or illness as an amazing opportunity to grow. I welcome them and I'm standing more upright now, willing to ask for what I want and speak up when I don't get it. The more I change, the easier it gets and the more comfortable I feel. I approach life much more gently, as my new perception has made me realise I don't have anything to push or force to get what I desire. I just ask and allow my request to come into my life. I haven't got everything I want yet, but I can at least see why and how I can adjust to change this. I watch as my life unravels and know that I am getting all that I attract by my expectations.

Anusha has made this change possible for me. It is a constant, powerful tool I have, to use whenever I feel the need. I have found the controls on my roller coaster and can now determine the speed in which I move forwards and to some extent the direction in which I go. I am always careful not to push too hard, to soften my approach to everything and allow life to take me in a direction that I find was not what I expected, but is exactly what I asked for.

Like an open, expectant child I find life is wondrous, full of amazing experiences and a joy to experience. And then one day it all goes wrong and I feel bogged down in my circumstances. I then stop and breathe, reminding myself who I am, or want to be and what I want to achieve and act accordingly. I release any tension, especially around my stomach/solar plexus, drop my shoulders and start again. I discover the reigns are back in my hands and I smile.

I have used at least one of the symbols every single day since I started on this journey and can't imagine not using them. They keep me in touch with what I want and who I really am when you peel away all the layers that I have created to supposedly protect me from the world. Anusha is a way of life and reduces any build up of blocked energy that you create and gives you the strength and vision to chip away at the barriers you have erected and release the patterns of behaviour and beliefs that no longer serve you.

Where will I go next? I can only just wait to find out. I do know that Anusha will always be a part of my life.

Sally is a Reiki /Anusha Master Teacher and Reiki Drum Practitioner working in Rickmansworth,

Hertfordshire. You can contact Sally at sallypage@tesco.net

SUSE SHARES

Anusha crept softly into my life a few years ago. I first heard about it indirectly when talking to a Reiki Master friend of mine. I was talking about moving back to Wycombe and how I felt that I didn't really fit in here, but had had to move back into the area due to life circumstances. As we discussed this, she mentioned that there seemed to be a group of people, who had previously been Essenes in other lives long ago, gathering and reconnecting in this area. I don't think I'd ever heard of the Essenes but I had a very emotional response to this. The name seemed familiar, tears came to my eyes, and the hairs on my arms stood up. Maybe there was more behind me moving back. I made a mental note to find out more.

It was some time later that I came across Anusha again. A healer friend of mine was giving me a healing, which was very powerful and emotional for me. Towards the end, I became overwhelmed with feelings of total bliss and love and felt myself become so light that I felt like I was flying out of the window through the top of my head! My friend asked me to try and describe how I was feeling and the words 'coming home' just popped into my head, so that's what I said! After the healing, she explained to me that she had used the Anusha Master symbol on my crown chakra, which is said to promote, among other things, a sense of coming home.

After such an amazing experience I felt I had to find out more about Anusha. I was already attuned to Reiki level II, but up to now hadn't really thought about taking this any further, but I couldn't ignore the incredible feeling of Anusha and decided to attend a Level I workshop.

During the day of the at-one-ment, we were given the opportunity to use and experience the different symbols. I was so struck by the fact that I could really feel the energy as I'd never been able to before, but not only that, each of the symbols had a totally different feel to them. During the weeks that followed, every time I used a symbol on someone for healing, they could feel something, whether they were particularly sensitive to energies or not. I have used Anusha on people who are Reiki healers themselves and can definitely distinguish the energy as different from Reiki – 'scintillating', 'electric', 'fizzy' are some of the words used. I've also used Anusha on people with no prior experience of energy healing who can feel the energy strongly.

Having recently reached Master Teacher level I can look over the last few years and see how far I've come on my spiritual journey since Anusha came into my life. Having wanted to be a healer for many years, but never really believing I was, I now feel empowered, strong and confident enough to truly walk my path as a healer and have finally reached a stage where I believe I can help people. Through the use of the Anusha symbols on a daily basis, I have found the strength to come out of hiding and be myself, to process and work through the emotions and self talk that have held me back so far in my life, to truly connect to divine love. I am gradually becoming more sensitive and open to higher energies, have had some experience of channelling and have clearly felt the presence of higher beings supporting and guiding me. My life seems to be more in the 'flow', more synchronicitous. I look upon my life from a higher, wider, more positive, perspective. For me though, the most intriguing aspect has been the Essene connection, and the reconnection, and sharing of recollections from hundreds of years ago, mainly through past life regressions, with very old, dear friends. This has given me more of a sense of purpose and meaning in my life.

Anusha has become a background to my everyday life, changing it subtly forever, and the small jigsaw pieces are slowly fitting together to make sense of everything that has gone before and is happening now. I really do feel like I am finally coming home.

Susan (Suse) Campbell is an Anusha Master Teacher, Reiki Level III and a Hypno-psychotherapist DHP (NC). Suse's mobile number is 07896 305839.

YOUR STORY

I wonder what your story will be around Anusha? If you've felt moved, fascinated, intrigued, inspired by anything you've read here, then please make contact with us. If you've felt a connection to angels, Jesus, the Essenes, the six-pointed star, Shiva Lingams or anything else that you've read about, then please contact us. Please do receive an at-one-ment to this beautiful energy. Join our community. We welcome you with open hearts and profound love.

You can contact us at **www.anushahealing.co.uk**

RECOMMENDED READING

Many of these authors are extremely prolific and have written books on numerous aspects of spirituality and metaphysics. I have chosen to mention here those books that especially inspired me on my Anusha journey.

A Harmony of Angels by Angela McGerr

All Love: A Guidebook for healing with Sekhem-Seichim-Reiki and SKHM by Diane Ruth Shewmaker

Angel Therapy: Healing Messages for Every Area of Your Life by Doreen Virtue

Archangels and Ascended Masters: A Guide to Working and Healing with Divinities and Deities by Doreen Virtue

Awaken Your Goddess: A Practical Guide to Discovering a Woman's Power, A Woman's Glory by Liz Simpson

Conversations with God by Neale Donald Walsch

Diary of a Psychic by Sonia Choquette

Eastern Body Western Mind: Psychology and the Chakra system as a Path to the Self by Anodea Judith

Essential Reiki by Diane Stein

Recommended Reading

From Enoch To The Dead Sea Scrolls by Edmond Bordeaux Szekely

Good Vibrations: Psychic Protection, Energy Enhancement and Space Clearing by Judy Hall

How My Death Saved My Life by Denise Lynn

How to be Happy: Finding a Future in Your Past by Jenny Smedley

Jesus and the Essenes by Dolores Cannon

Life Between Lives: Hypnotherapy for Spiritual Regression by Michael Newton

Listening to Trees by Thea Holly

Many Lives, Many Masters by Brian Weiss

Praying Peace by James F. Twyman (in conversation with Gregg Braden and Doreen Virtue)

Radical Forgiveness: Making Way for The Miracle by Colin C. Tipping

Reiki For Life: The Complete Guide to Reiki Practice for Levels 1, 2 & 3 by Penelope Quest

Reiki: The Legacy of Dr. Usui by Frank Arjava Petter

Serpent of Light: Beyond 2012 by Drunvalo Melchizedek

Soul Angels: How to Find your Angels by Jenny Smedley

Stillness Speaks by Eckhart Tolle

Tera, My Journey Home by Kathleen Ann Milner

RECOMMENDED READING

The Age of Miracles: Embracing the New Midlife by Marianne Williamson

The Ancient Secret of the Flower of Life Vols 1 & 2 by Drunvalo Melchizedek

The Art of Spiritual Peacemaking: Secret Teachings from Jeshua ben Joseph by James F. Twyman

The Crystal Bible: A Definitive Guide to Crystals by Judy Hall

The Essenes: Children of the Light by Stuart Wilson and Joanna Prentis

The Four Agreements by Don Miguel Ruiz

The Gospel of the Essenes by Edmond Bordeaux Szekely

The Little Book of Starlight by White Eagle

The Prayer of St. Francis by James F. Twyman

The Seven Spiritual Laws of Success by Deepak Chopra

Tuesdays With Morrie by Mitch Albom

2012 and Beyond: An Invitation to Meet the Challenges and Opportunities Ahead by Diana Cooper

Waiting for Autumn by Scott Blum

You Can Heal Your Life by Louise Hay

Your Soul's Plan by Robert Schwartz

Zero Limits: The Secret Hawaiian System for Wealth, Health, Peace, and More by Joe Vitale and Ihaleakala Hew Len

GRATITUDE

I am deeply and profoundly grateful to the following people:

Kate, to whom I extend deepest love and appreciation, without whom Anusha healing nor this book would exist.

My parents, sister and brother for their loving support, acceptance and encouragement.

My children and grandchildren, who are a constant source of love, hope, joy and inspiration.

My publisher, Murielle, for her empowering and enthusiastic support.

Greg Pike for his breathtaking cover design, internal artwork and photography.

My editorial team of Frankie, Lesley, Liz M, Suse and Vince for their dedicated and sterling work in spotting all the errors and adding their magic!

Neens, Tommo, Frankie and Jules F for their invaluable, sensitive and loving feedback on the first chapter and for highlighting that I'm the exclamation mark Queen!!!

Colin Tipping, Jenny Smedley, Judy Hall, Julia Webb-Harvey, LeelaLight, Sarah Lewis, Thea Holly... Barbara, Frankie, Giles, Helen E, Liz E, Liz M and Vince for writing such gracious and generous reviews.

Dolores Cannon and Ozark Mountain Publishing, Inc for permission to use the picture of Qumran from the book 'Jesus and The Essenes'.

Colin Tipping, Judy Hall and Thea Holly, for permission to quote from their material.

Angela McGerr, Amarna Sinclair and LeelaLight for permission to share our experiences of their workshops.

All those contributors to websites, articles etc. that have inspired and informed me during this extensive journey.

Darryl, Debbie A, Ian, Judith Cl, Lesley, Liz E, Liz M, Natalie, Pat, Rita, Sally and Suse for contributing their fascinating and inspiring experiences.

GRATITUDE

Frankie for her stunning visualisation and Lesley for her wonder-ful invocations.

My dearest 'sis', Jules and all the special people with whom the Anusha symbols came through.

The entire Anusha community, all those beautiful souls who I've been blessed to reconnect with, all those whose combined love and light brought through this extraordinary energy, all those who are committed to heal themselves and others and, in doing so, are changing the world for the better (Master Teachers in bold):

Amanda, Amelie, Andy, **Anna**, Annie, **Barbara**, Bob, Claire, Darryl, **Debbie A**, Debbie S, Edith, **Frankie**, Freya, Giles, Greg, Gwyneth, Helen C, Helen E, Ian, Jacqui, James, John, Judith Ca, **Judith Cl**, Jules F, Kacie, **Katy**, Kuryan, Layla, **Lesley**, Linda, **Lindsay**, **Liz E**, **Liz M**, Lynn, Maria, Murielle, Natalie, Niamh, **Nikki**, Pam, **Pat**, Paula, Priahw, Priscilla, Rita, Ros, **Sally**, Sarah H, Sarah S, Sooz, Sophie, Sue C, Sue K, **Suse**, Steph, Stephanie, Tarrick, Tom, Trish, Vince, Viviana, Yvonne, Zan.

Lastly, I express my heartfelt thanks to the Spiritual Beings who guide, support and inspire me through every moment of my life, who facilitated the emergence of Anusha and 'held me' lovingly as I wrote.

About the Author

Patsi has dedicated her adult life to empowering others to develop and grow, to teaching and healing in its many forms. She began this journey as a Lecturer in Further Education, passionately teaching an array of subjects from Mathematics to Sociology. After a gruelling, yet inspiring, three-year stint teaching at an Institute for Young Offenders, Patsi became ill with ME. She identifies this period of pain and loss as one of the best things that ever happened to her, presenting an opportunity to review her life and appreciate what truly matters.

As her health gradually improved, she chose to focus on counselling, working with disadvantaged young people and vulnerable women. She became the Co-ordinator of a counselling agency for people with mental health issues then Development Worker, first at a Youth Counselling Agency and later at a Rape Crisis Centre.

At some point, she made a decision to devote her energy to developing herself, which involved becoming attuned to Reiki, and her fascinating and enlightening journey as a healer began. This journey has taken her from being a Reiki Master Teacher, attuning hundreds of healers, through being attuned to Karuna and Sekhem, until everything synthesised together and Anusha presented itself.

Patsi says that Anusha has shone a beacon of love and light on her life, guiding, supporting and inspiring her to reconnect with herself and others and to fully realise that we are all connected as one. She sincerely hopes that it fills your life with love and light and takes you to a place of peace and fulfilment.

ABOUT KATE

Kate works as a Psychodynamic Counsellor, Healer and Group Facilitator. She experienced bereavement counselling many years ago, which led her to train as a counsellor and started her on her healing path. She is a Reiki and Karuna Master, Sehkem Level 2 and, of course, was responsible with Patsi for bringing through the Anusha Healing energy.

Patsi and Kate enjoy working together at The Winters Way Therapy Centre. For more information please visit www.anushahealing.co.uk

INDEX

238

Lightning Source UK Ltd.
Milton Keynes UK
UKOW020656170212

187451UK00001B/19/P